Your Rights on the Job

A Practical Guide to Employment Laws in Massachusetts

Fifth Edition

By Robert M. Schwartz

Drawings by Nick Thorkelson

The Labor Guild of Boston

Weymouth, Massachusetts

Printed in the United States of America
ISBN 978-0-9611038-4-2
Library of Congress Number: 2008902335

Design and production by Nick Thorkelson

The Labor Guild of Boston
85 Commercial St.
Weymouth, Massachusetts 01188
781-340-7887

Dedicated to Edward F. Boyle S.J.

1931-2007

Longtime chaplain of the Labor Guild of Boston.

A toiler in the vineyard of social change and a true friend to all who strive for justice and fairness in the workplace

Contents

Publisher's Note

The Labor Guild of Boston is pleased to have a part in the publication and distribution of *Your Rights on the Job*, a scholarly and popular treatment of the legal aspects of work in Massachusetts. The Guild is a membership group whose School of Industrial Relations aims to help men and women act with conscience, know-how, and courage in labor-management relations.

Robert M. Schwartz, the author of this book, is an outstanding member of our faculty. He brings to his writing the expertise and wisdom that come from day-to-day involvement in the field, and a happy facility for presenting the technical and legal realities of labor relations in straightforward language.

Your Rights on the Job is a comprehensive treatment of state and federal labor laws. It lends itself to frequent reference by union and nonunion employees, labor union officers, management personnel, industrial relations representatives, lawyers, academics, arbitrators, public agency officials, and other members of the community served by the Labor Guild.

Preface

This book explains the rights of Massachusetts workers and suggests ways to enforce those rights. I thought of it while working for the Massachusetts Labor Relations Commission (now the Division of Labor Relations). Taking telephone calls from the public, I discovered that the laws, regulations, and court decisions governing work in our commonwealth were poorly known and difficult to access.

When I left the commission in 1981, I determined to write a manual that workers could rely on in dealing with management, government agencies, and the courts. I was delighted when The Labor Guild of Boston, a leader in worker education in Massachusetts, agreed to sponsor the project. The first edition of *Your Rights on the Job* was published in 1983.

This edition is current to July 2008. Developments since the fourth edition include:

- Higher minimum wage rates
- New rules defining independent contractors
- Longer filing periods at the Massachusetts Commission Against Discrimination
- A ban on smoking in the workplace
- Prohibitions on genetic testing

- New health insurance requirements
- Changes in unemployment insurance for temporary employees
- New procedures for union organizing in the public sector

Several persons generously gave of their time and expertise to help me prepare this edition. I would particularly like to thank Marsha Hunter of the Massachusetts Office of the Attorney General, Lisa Price of the Massachusetts Division of Occupational Safety, Monica Halas of Greater Boston Legal Services, attorney Alan S. Pierce, and the attorneys of Sandulli Grace P.C.

Introduction

A vast array of laws govern wage payments, leaves, safety, organizing, discrimination, and other workplace concerns. Extensive regulations also apply, issued by the U.S. Department of Labor, the Equal Employment Opportunity Commission, the Massachusetts Commission Against Discrimination, and other agencies. Court opinions and administrative decisions further swell the corpus of labor law. Creating an element of confusion, Massachusetts and the federal government sometimes enact laws on the same subject. Generally, the better standard controls, although sometimes federal law takes precedence. Another frustration: some laws exempt small businesses and government employers.

Learning about labor law is similar to solving a jigsaw puzzle. At first the bits of knowledge appear scattered and overwhelming. After a while you begin to perceive a logic and interconnectedness. Eventually the picture takes shape.

Obtaining Laws

As you read *Your Rights on the Job*, you may come across some laws that you want to have in their entirety; perhaps to show to coworkers or to your employer. In previous editions I suggested public libraries. The internet has since emerged as a more convenient resource.

Legal archives are available on the following websites:

Massachusetts laws: www.mass.gov/legis/laws/mgl/mgllink.htm
Massachusetts regulations: www.lawlib.state.ma.us/cmr.html
Federal laws: www4.law.cornell.edu/uscode
Federal regulations: www.gpoaccess.gov/cfr/retrieve.html

Endnotes

The notes at the back of the book provide the legal citations for the laws discussed in the text. They also contain supplemental information. To keep the numbers reasonable, the notes are limited to specifically mentioned laws, controversial areas, and matters about which employers may be skeptical.

Government Agencies

Employees can often enforce their rights by filing complaints at governmental agencies such as the U.S. Department of Labor or the Massachusetts Commission Against Discrimination (MCAD). Complaint forms are available on agency websites.

Complainants should closely monitor their cases. Many agencies are understaffed and can use help to locate witnesses, documents, and other evidence. If an agency drags its feet, call or write the agency's director or an elected official.

There are other ways to speed up investigations. A few years ago, eight hundred Quincy shipyard workers signed a discrimination complaint and delivered it *en masse* to the MCAD. Within weeks the agency persuaded the employer to end its illegal practices.

Lawsuits

Many labor laws—such as Title VII, the Family and Medical Leave Act, and the Massachusetts Wage Act—allow workers to sue in court instead of depending on an agency to take action. Names of lawyers who specialize in labor law are available from the National Lawyers Guild, the American Civil Liberties Union of Massachusetts, the National Employment Lawyers Association, and the Massachusetts Bar Association. Legal service agencies also take labor cases.

Lawyers work hardest for clients who stay on top of their cases. Call your attorney regularly, and ask for copies of your papers.

Two Worlds

Although union and nonunion employers are generally subject to the same labor laws, the ability of workers to insist on compliance varies dramatically.

Protected by collective bargaining agreements, grievance-arbitration procedures, and the power of group solidarity, the commonwealth's 400,000 union workers can aggressively demand that their legal rights be respected. Moreover, due to their contracts, union workers often have rights that exceed those provided by state and federal laws.

Workers without union representation, "at-will employees," are not so lucky. Even though most of the labor laws forbid retaliation, an at-will employee who asserts a legal entitlement takes a substantial risk. Even requesting a personnel file, a right unambiguously guaranteed by state law, can be dangerous.

These realities do not make *Your Rights on the Job* irrelevant to the state's 2.5 million nonunion workers. In some areas, such as safety and health, government agencies investigate without revealing complainants' names. In other areas, such as unemployment benefits and workers' compensation, retaliation may not be a pressing consideration. Nevertheless, the most important part of this book for at-will employees may well be Chapter 6, which explains how to organize a union.

Chapter One

You Earned It

▶ Paychecks
▶ Overtime Pay
▶ Minimum Wages
▶ Prevailing Wages

O pening your pay envelope to find less than expected is always a shock. Of course, you may have overestimated your earnings. Another possibility is that your employer is holding back money you are entitled to receive.

PAYCHECKS

The Massachusetts Wage Act, enacted in 1886, requires employers to pay wages promptly, fully, and regularly.[1] Criminal and civil penalties apply.

In Brief
The Massachusetts Wage Act

COVERED EMPLOYEES
- Private sector workers, including persons working for nonprofit organizations[2]
- Government workers[3]

EXCLUDED
- Independent contractors[4]

MAJOR PROVISIONS
- Wages, salaries, and commissions must be paid within six days of when pay periods close.
- Discharged employees must be paid in full on their final day.

ENFORCEMENT AGENCY
- Fair Labor Division of the Office of the Massachusetts Attorney General (see addresses and telephone numbers on page 153)

PENALTIES
- A criminal prosecution can be brought against a president, treasurer, managing officer, managing agent, or responsible public official.[5]
- A civil penalty of up to $25,000 can be assessed if a violation is intentional; up to $10,000 if it is unintentional.
- Employees can sue for triple damages plus legal expenses.

ADDITIONAL INFORMATION
- Employers may not fire or otherwise retaliate against employees who complain about wage violations or file charges with the attorney general.
- The wage act applies to undocumented immigrants.
- Unionized employees may not be able to use the wage act if the amount owed requires interpretation of a collective bargaining agreement.[6]

• Employers may not, by special agreements or contracts, exempt themselves from compliance.[7]

Deadlines

Employees who are employed five or six days a week must be paid within six days of the close of the pay period during which wages are earned. Employees who work seven days a week must be paid within seven days. Employees who work fewer than five days must be paid within seven days of the last day worked.

> **EXAMPLE:** The pay period at Acme Floors runs from Sunday to Saturday. Acme must issue paychecks no later than the following Friday.

Holding back or deferring wages is illegal, even if the employee "consents." An employer that is short of funds must borrow or make other arrangements to meet the deadline.

Paychecks must include all wages, salary, overtime, bonuses, and incentive pay earned during the pay period. Commissions must also be paid by the deadline — if they are arithmetically determinable, and due under company policies.[8]

Frequency

Hourly workers must be paid on a weekly or biweekly basis. Salaried executive, administrative, and professional employees can be paid weekly, biweekly, semimonthly or, if the employee requests, monthly. An employee absent on payday must be paid on demand.

Method of payment. Wages may be paid by cash or check.[9] Promissory notes or IOUs are illegal. Employers must provide free check cashing at a bank or elsewhere. Payslips, check stubs, or pay envelopes must list the name of the employer, the name of the employee, the date, the number of hours worked, the hourly rate, and any deductions or additions.[9]

Final Paychecks

Employees who are discharged must be paid in full on their final day. Employees who quit, retire, or leave employment for other reasons must be paid in full on their next regular payday. Final paychecks must include vacation and holiday earnings due under company policies.[10]

Deductions

Deductions are limited to the following:
- State and federal taxes
- Social Security contributions (FICA)
- Pension contributions
- Insurance premiums
- Vacation, health, and welfare fund contributions
- Credit union assessments
- Union dues
- Wage garnishments authorized by court order
- Meals and lodging (see page 30)
- Penalties for lateness (see below)
- Penalties for shortages (see below)

Lateness. Penalties for lateness may not exceed time lost.

EXAMPLE: Bernice Allen earns $10 per hour. If she is thirty minutes late, $5 can be deducted from her paycheck.

Shortages. Employers may hold back wages due to a "valid setoff."[11] Although the wage act does not define this term, the enforcing authorities sometimes apply it to a cash or property shortage for which the jobholder is solely responsible. A setoff may not be taken if it reduces weekly pay below the minimum wage level.

Poor performance or damage to company property are not valid grounds for wage setoffs.

AG Complaint

Employees can file wage act complaints with the attorney general's Fair Labor Division. Forms are available on the attorney general's website. Supporting information must be attached.

The division contacts the employer, attempts to resolve the matter, and determines whether to prosecute, issue a civil citation, or seek restitution.[12] If the division fails to resolve the matter, the employee can swear out a criminal complaint or bring a private lawsuit. If the company goes out of business, employees can sue the president, treasurer, managing officer, or managing agent, or file claims in bankruptcy court.

OVERTIME PAY

The federal Fair Labor Standards Act (FLSA) and the Massachusetts Overtime Act require employers to pay wages at a rate of time-and-one-half for hours that exceed forty in a seven-day workweek.[13] Overtime premiums must be calculated weekly, even if pay periods are longer. For example, an employee paid biweekly who works forty-eight hours the first week of a pay period and thirty-two hours the next is due eight hours of overtime pay.[14] Employers (other than state agencies) do not have to pay premiums for hours that exceed eight in a day. Nor is extra pay required for weekend or night work.

In Brief
Federal and State Overtime Laws

COVERED EMPLOYEES
- Private sector workers
- Government workers

EXCLUDED EMPLOYEES
- Executive, administrative, professional, and outside sales employees
- Employees of seasonal (open fewer than 121 days per year) businesses holding federal and state exemption permits
- Seafarers, fishers, and agricultural workers
- Railway and air carrier workers
- Drivers of commercial motor vehicles engaged in interstate commerce and their helpers[15]

MAJOR PROVISION
- Employees must be paid 1.5 times their regular rates for hours worked in excess of forty in a workweek.

ENFORCEMENT AGENCIES
- Wage and Hour Division of the U.S. Department of Labor (see page 156)
- Fair Labor Division of the Office of the Massachusetts Attorney General (see page 153)

PENALTIES
An employer may be ordered to:
- Pay triple back overtime plus interest
- Pay a fine of up to $50,000
- Serve a jail sentence of up to two years

ADDITIONAL INFORMATION
- Employers may not retaliate against employees who complain about overtime violations, file complaints, or sue in court.
- Employers must retain records of daily and weekly hours worked for at least two years and allow inspections by employees at reasonable times and places.[16]

White-Collar Exemptions

Executive, administrative, professional, and outside sales employees are exempt from the overtime requirements. Exempt employees may be assigned unlimited hours without additional compensation.

To qualify as exempt, employees must be paid at least $455 per week and satisfy the factors described below. Other than physicians, lawyers, teachers, outside salespersons, and employees in certain computer-related occupations, employees must be paid on a salary basis. Except for computer and outside sales employees, workers paid by the hour are not exempt whatever their income or duties.

Executives. Employees qualify as executives if they are paid a salary of $455 or more per week and meet three requirements:

1. The employee's primary duty (occupying at least half the workweek) is managing an enterprise or a recognized department or subdivision of an enterprise.[17]

2. The employee directs the work of at least two full-time employees or their equivalent.

3. The employee has the authority to hire or fire, or the employer gives the employee's recommendations particular weight.

Employees whose annual compensation is $100,000 or more are exempt if they meet one of the above requirements and do not perform manual work.

Administrative employees. Employees qualify as administrative if they are paid on a salary or fee basis at a rate of $455 or more per week and meet two requirements:

1. The employee's primary duty is the performance of work directly related to management policies or general business operations. Examples include positions in finance, budgeting, auditing, quality control, and purchasing.

2. The employee exercises significant discretion and independent judgment with respect to matters of significance.

Employees whose annual compensation is $100,000 or more are exempt if they meet one of the above requirements and do not perform manual work.

Professionals. The professional exemption has two categories: learned and creative.

Learned professionals. Learned professionals are exempt if they are paid on a salary or fee basis at a rate of $455 or more per week and meet three requirements:

1. The employee's primary duty is the performance of intellectual work requiring advanced knowledge and the consistent exercise of discretion and judgment. Examples include teachers, lawyers, and doctors.

2. The advanced knowledge is in a field of science or learning.

3. The advanced knowledge is acquired by a prolonged course of specialized intellectual instruction.

Employees whose annual compensation is $100,000 or more are exempt if they meet one of the above requirements.

Creative professionals. Creative professionals are exempt if they are paid on a salary or fee basis at a rate of $455 or more per week for work requiring invention, imagination, originality, or talent in a recognized artistic or creative field. Examples include actors, musicians, and composers.

Computer workers. Systems analysts, programmers, software engineers, and other highly proficient computer professionals are exempt if they are paid $455 or more per week on a salary or fee basis, or $27.63 or more in hourly wages.[18]

Outside sales employees. Outside sales employees are exempt if their primary duties are making sales or obtaining orders and they are regularly engaged away from the employer's place of business.

Exempt and nonexempt. The table on the opposite page lists positions usually classified as exempt or nonexempt. In reviewing the table, understand that job titles do not determine whether an exemption applies and that employers must evaluate duties on a case-by-case basis.

Computing Overtime Pay

Nonexempt workers must be paid 1.5 times their "regular rate" for each overtime hour. The calculation of the regular rate depends on how the employee is paid.

Hourly rate. When an employee is paid solely on an hourly basis —without incentive pay, commissions, or bonuses—the regular rate is the hourly rate.

Hourly rate plus additional earnings. When an hourly worker has additional cash earnings such as incentive pay, shift differentials, or on-call pay, the regular rate is determined by dividing total straight-time earnings by the number of hours worked.[19]

> EXAMPLE: Sandra Mills worked 50 hours at $10 per hour. In addition, she earned $100 in incentive pay. Her straight-time earnings are $600. Her regular rate for the week is $12 ($600 ÷ 50 hours). Her hourly overtime premium is $6 (half of $12). Her total overtime premium is $60 ($6 x 10 hours). In all, she is due $660.

Holiday pay, sick pay, travel expenses, disability benefits, and employer contributions to pension or health insurance plans are not included in the regular rate.

OVERTIME EXEMPTIONS

	Exempt (need not be paid for overtime)	Nonexempt (must be paid for overtime)
Executive	Personnel manager Fire captain Department head Store manager Construction project superintendent	Working foreperson Management trainee Group leader Police sergeant Fire lieutenant
Administrative	Vice principal Credit manager Safety director Marketing director Systems analyst Human relations manager Buyer Executive assistant	Bank teller Union field staff Bookkeeper Secretary Sales representative Dietician Computer operator Personnel clerk Inspector Customer service representative IT support specialist
Professional	Doctor Lawyer Accountant Teacher Registered nurse Nurse practitioner Dental hygienist Engineer Physician assistant Executive or sous chef Certified medical technologist Newspaper columnist Actor	Accounts clerk Day care provider X-ray technician Junior engineer Drafter Licensed practical nurse Cook Photographer Paralegal Newspaper reporter Radiology technician Corrections officer Firefighter Police officer

Piecework. The regular rate of an employee paid on a piecework basis is earnings divided by hours worked. The overtime premium is 50 percent of the regular rate for each hour over forty.

EXAMPLE: Maxine Booth worked 45 hours. Her piecework earnings are $900. Her regular rate for the week is $20 ($900 ÷ 45 hours). Her hourly overtime premium is $10. She is due $50 in overtime pay. In all, she is due $950.

NOTE: Another acceptable method is to pay 1.5 times the piece rate for each piece produced during overtime hours.

Retroactive bonus. If a bonus payment is based on work going back longer than the current pay period, the employer must recompute overtime compensation.

EXAMPLE: Johnson Paper paid an end-of-year bonus of $1,000. Employees who worked overtime during the year are entitled to additional payments equal to the bonus divided by the number of hours worked, multiplied by one-half, further multiplied by the overtime hours.

NOTE: Bonuses paid solely at the discretion of the employer are treated as gifts and do not require additional overtime pay. Bonuses based on hours worked, production, profits, efficiency, or a union contract are not gifts.

Retroactive pay. An employer that awards a retroactive pay increase may have to recalculate overtime. For example, an increase of $1.00 per hour going back three months requires an additional $.50 for each overtime hour.

Compensatory time. Private sector employers in Massachusetts cannot substitute compensatory time off for required overtime compensation.[20]

Compensatory time practices are permissible in the public sector if employees are allowed 1.5 hours of time off for each hour of overtime. Employees must be allowed to use the hours on request, unless an absence will unduly disrupt operations.[21]

Salaried workers. Computing overtime pay for nonexempt salaried workers—for example, secretaries, newspaper reporters, and paralegals—depends on whether the employer and the worker have

a fluctuating or a fixed workweek agreement.

Fluctuating workweek agreement. An agreement that a salary covers all straight-time hours is a fluctuating workweek agreement. To compute overtime pay, the salary is divided by the number of hours worked. Since the salary covers straight-time pay for all hours, the employer need only pay an additional 50 percent of the regular rate for the hours that exceed forty.

EXAMPLE: Paula Hart was hired as a secretary with the understanding that her $700 salary would cover her straight-time pay for all hours worked. Her usual schedule is 35 hours. If Hart works 8 hours Saturday, she is due pay for the week as follows: Her regular rate is $16.28 ($700 ÷ 43 hours). Her overtime premium is $8.14. She is due $24.42 for the 3 hours over 40, making her pay for the week $724.42.

NOTE: If Hart works 5 hours on Saturday, she is not due any extra pay, as her hours for the week do not exceed 40.

Fixed workweek agreement. Employees who are hired with an understanding that their salary is for a maximum number of hours have a fixed workweek agreement. To compute overtime, salary is divided by scheduled hours. Time-and-one-half this rate must be paid for each hour that exceeds forty.

EXAMPLE: Bookkeeper Paul Harris earns a salary of $700 for a fixed 35-hour week. If he works 43 hours, he is entitled to pay as follows: His salary is $700. His regular rate is $20 ($700 ÷ 35 hours). He is due this rate for the hours between 35 and 40.[22] He is due $30 for each hour that exceeds 40. For the week he is due $890 ($700 plus $100 plus $90).

As the examples demonstrate, workers who have fixed workweek agreements earn higher pay for the same number of hours. Unfortunately for employees, the Department of Labor and the courts almost always classify salaries as fluctuating agreements.

Compensable Time

Calculating overtime pay requires an accurate tally of work hours. The Department of Labor defines work as all time during which an employee is required to be on the employer's premises, to be on duty, or to be at a prescribed worksite.[23]

Work outside scheduled hours. In addition to regular hours, employers must count nonscheduled activities that:

1. Are undertaken primarily for the employer's benefit; and

2. Are performed with the knowledge of the employer, or so openly that the employer should have reason to know about them; and

3. Are not prohibited by the employer.[24]

Compensable hours includes pre- and post-shift meetings, giving report, and working at home. An employee's failure to obtain prior authorization to work outside scheduled hours, or a failure to report work on timecards, is not grounds to treat the time as noncompensable—if management was aware that the employee was working and there was no intent on the employee's part to mislead or deceive.[25]

Meal periods. Bona fide meal periods are not compensable if employees are completely relieved of both active and inactive duties for the purpose of eating a regular meal.[26] Employees must be allowed to leave the premises.[27] If meals are constantly interrupted or if employees must keep watch over the premises, the time must be counted. Rest periods and coffee breaks are compensable.

Travel and commuting time. An employee who must travel from one place of work to another during the work day, for example a home health aide who works at several residences, must be compensated for travel time.[28] Regular commuting between home and work is generally not treated as work time.[29]

On-call time. On-call time usually does not qualify as work time—even if the employee has to carry a pager or a cell phone. An exception applies if the employer's demands are so intrusive that the employee is unable to use the time for personal enjoyment; for example, if call-backs are frequent or if employees must stay near the workplace.

Sleeping time. If an employee is allowed to nap or sleep while on duty at the worksite, the hours count as work time. However, if the employee is required to be on the premises for twenty-four hours or

THE INDEPENDENT CONTRACTOR GAME

Employers are increasingly hiring workers as "independent contractors," "consultants," and "freelancers." In some cases, the motive is to avoid paying overtime, prevailing wages, workers' compensation, and unemployment insurance. In other cases it is to prevent union organizing. The practice is widespread in the construction, personal services, and technology industries.

Many of these employers are in violation of the Massachusetts Independent Contractor Misclassification Statute.[30] This law says that a person who provides a service for pay must be treated as an employee unless:

1. The service is performed with independence and autonomy, free from the hiring entity's control and direction; and

2. The service is outside the usual course of the hiring entity's business; and

3. The person is engaged in an independently established trade, occupation, profession, or business of the same nature as that involved in the service performed.

The second test is especially difficult. It bars an employer from classifying a worker as a contractor if the worker performs tasks similar to those performed by the employer's regular employees, or if the worker provides services that the entity regularly provides. A painting company, for example, must treat painters as employees even if they are paid by the job.

A business's failure to withhold income taxes, provide workers' compensation, or make unemployment insurance payments does not make an employee a contractor. Nor does a written contract.

Employers who improperly classify employees, and in doing so violate the wage payment, overtime, minimum wage, prevailing wage, or workers' compensation laws, risk additional criminal and civil penalties.[31] They may also be debarred from public works projects.[32]

more, a regularly scheduled sleeping period of up to eight hours can be excluded
unless conditions are such that the
employee cannot get a reasonable night's
sleep.[33]

Work at home. Work at home is compensable if the employer assigns it or is
aware of the activity.

Classes. Classes, lectures, and training
programs are compensable if they are
required by the employer or if they are
job related.

Grievance time. Investigating and discussing union grievances
during the work day counts as work time unless exempted by a collective bargaining agreement or by consistent past practice.[34]

Back Pay

Union workers can generally obtain redress for overtime infractions
through their contractual grievance and arbitration procedures. Nonunion employees can file complaints with the U.S. Department of
Labor (DOL) or the state fair labor division. DOL investigates without revealing the name of the complainant.

Another option is to sue. Under the state overtime act, a court can
award triple back pay plus legal expenses. Employees can file lawsuits up to two years after violations, but are advised to act sooner as
each week of delay may cancel a week of back wages.[35]

MINIMUM WAGES

Both the federal government and Massachusetts enforce minimum
wage standards. As of July 24, 2008, the Massachusetts standard was
$8.00 per hour while the federal standard was $6.55.[36] The federal
standard rises to $7.25 on July 24, 2009. In the private sector, the
state standard takes precedence. In the government and agricultural
sectors, the federal standard applies.[37] Compliance is judged on a
weekly basis: If a worker is paid $320 for a forty-hour week, there is
no violation even if some hours are not compensated.

In Brief
Federal and State Minimum Wage Laws

COVERED EMPLOYEES
- Full- and part-time workers, including casual and seasonal workers

EXCLUDED EMPLOYEES
- Professional employees, outside sales persons, participants in certain training and rehabilitation programs, inmates working in prison

MAJOR PROVISIONS
- Private sector employers must pay employees—including part-timers and teenagers—at least $8.00 per hour.
- Public agencies must pay employees at least $6.55 per hour as of July 24, 2008 and $7.25 per hour as of July 24, 2009.
- Tipped employees must be paid at least $2.63 per hour.

ENFORCEMENT AGENCIES
- Fair Labor Division of the Office of the Attorney General (see page 153)
- Wage and Hour Division of the U.S. Department of Labor (see page 156)

PENALTIES
An employer may be ordered to:
- Pay triple unpaid wages plus interest
- Pay a fine of up to $50,000
- Serve a jail sentence of up to two years

Tipped Employees

Tipped employees such as waitpersons, bartenders, cabdrivers, and bellhops may be paid cash wages of as little as $2.63 per hour.[38] This is known as the *service rate*. The difference between the service rate and the minimum wage is called the employer's *tip credit*. Service rates may only be paid if the following conditions apply:

1. The service rate plus tips at least matches the minimum wage for the week (earnings for a forty-hour employee must be at least $320). If business is slow or an employee has a poor week, the employer must pay additional wages to bring earnings to the minimum level.

2. The employer informs the employee of the amount of the tip credit and the employee's right to additional pay if gratuities are short.[39]

3. If patrons pay a service charge, or add a tip to a credit card payment, management distributes the gratuity in proportion to the services provided by the wait staff.[40]

4. Employees are allowed to retain all tips other than amounts contributed to a legitimate tip pool (see below).

Tip pool. Employers may require employees to pool their tips if the policy complies with the following rules:

1. After distributions to and from the pool, no employee is left with an unreasonable percentage of the tips received by that employee.[41]

2. Contributions do not cause total earnings to drop below the minimum wage.

3. Distributions are limited to waiters, counter staff, bus persons, bartenders, and other waitstaff employees.[42] Owners, managers, and supervisors may not take part, even if they serve food or drinks.

Retaliation. It is illegal to punish employees because they object to service-rate or tip-pool violations, or file complaints with the attorney general.[43]

Meals and Lodging

Pay deductions from minimum wage employees are closely regulated.

Meals. Employers that provide meals may deduct no more than $1.50 for breakfast, $2.25 for lunch, and $2.25 for dinner.[44]

Lodging. Employers that provide lodging can deduct no more than $35 per week for a one-person room, $30 per week for a two-person room, or $25 per week for a three-person room. The employee must request the room and use it.[45]

Uniforms. Employers may not charge for uniforms or laundering if this reduces weekly pay below minimum wage levels.[46]

Subminimums

Learners and apprentices may be paid 80 percent of the minimum wage with a license from the Massachusetts Division of Occupational Safety. Schools, colleges, hospitals, laboratories, and summer camps can apply for 80-percent licenses for the employment of students.

Show-up Pay

Employees who are scheduled for duty of three hours or more, show up at the time specified, but are sent home immediately or within three hours, must be paid an amount that is at least three times the Massachusetts minimum wage.[47] An example is a worker sent home early because of an electricity failure.

Living Wages

In recent years community and labor activists have campaigned for "living wage" ordinances that mandate higher wages for municipal workers and the employees of contractors doing municipal business. Boston, Brookline, Cambridge, and Somerville have responded. Wage levels are indexed to provide for yearly increases.

Boston. The Boston living wage, $12.20 per hour as of July 1, 2007, applies to contractors and subcontractors supplying $25,000 or more in services and to nonprofit organizations receiving city funding.

Brookline. The Brookline living wage, $10.70 per hour as of July 1, 2007, applies to businesses holding contracts with the town of $5,000 or more.

Cambridge. The Cambridge living wage, $12.98 per hour as of March 1, 2007, applies to the city, businesses supplying services to the city, and organizations receiving $10,000 or more in city funding.

Somerville. The Somerville living wage, $10.84 per hour as of July 1, 2007, applies to the city and to businesses supplying services to the city of $10,000 or more.

PREVAILING WAGES

State and federal "prevailing wage" laws require public works contractors and subcontractors to pay mechanics, drivers, and laborers (both skilled and unskilled) at rates corresponding to union wages in the geographic area.[48] The Massachusetts Division of Occupational Safety issues schedules for state projects. The U.S. Department of Labor issues schedules for federal projects. In some trades rates exceed $50 per hour.

Work covered by the prevailing wage laws includes:
- Construction, alteration, repair, and demolition of public buildings or structures
- Municipal trash collection
- Moving state offices
- Cleaning state buildings
- Printing state publications
- Transporting pupils
- Maintaining public housing

Violations

Employers violate the prevailing wage laws if they pay inadequate wages, place workers in incorrect trade categories, or misclassify employees as independent contractors. Violations should be reported to the attorney general's Fair Labor Division or the U.S. Department of Labor.[49]

Questions *and* Answers

Paid time off

Q. Are holidays or personal days counted when determining whether employees have worked more than forty hours in a week?

A. No. Paid time off does not qualify as hours worked.

Union contract

Q. Our union contract says that attendance at night training programs is to be compensated as straight pay. Does this overrule the FLSA requirement that overtime be paid at time-and-one half?

A. No. The FLSA supercedes inconsistent provisions in union contracts.[50]

Daily overtime

Q: Our company pays time-and-one-half when we work more than eight hours in a day, but only straight pay when we work on Saturdays. Violation?

A. Not necessarily. Premiums for daily overtime can be credited toward compensation due under the FLSA.[51]

Mandatory overtime

Q. Can manufacturers make employees work more than forty hours?

A: Yes. The only laws that prohibit mandatory overtime apply to retail stores on Sundays and holidays, and to work by minors.[52]

Unrequested work

Q. As a newspaper reporter, I often worked sixty or seventy hours a week on my stories—without receiving extra pay. Now that I have retired could I sue for back pay even though I was never told to work overtime and my hours were not recorded?

A. Yes, if you can prove that management knew or should have known that you were working the extra hours. You must also submit evidence that will enable a court to reasonably approximate the number of hours worked.

Garnishment

Q. My ex-wife is attaching my wages because I am behind in my child support. Can I be fired because of it?

A. No. An employer may not take adverse action because a court garnishes wages to satisfy a support order.[53]

Police

Q. Does the FSLA apply to police departments?

A. Yes, but unless required by a labor agreement, police and correctional departments do not have to pay overtime unless an officer's hours exceed 43 for a 7-day work period, 171 hours for a 28-day period, or a proportionate number of hours for a period between 7 and 28 days.[54]

Domestic work

Q. I perform live-in domestic service for a family in Newton. Sometimes I put in seventy hours. Should I be receiving time-and-one-half?

A. Yes. The state overtime law covers domestic service workers.[55]

Babysitters

Q. Do the minimum wage laws apply to babysitters?

A. Usually, no. Most qualify as independent contractors.

Camp counselors

Q. Do the minimum wage laws apply to camp counselors?

A. Yes, but if a camp secures a waiver from the Division of Occupational Safety, it can pay student workers 80 percent of the minimum wage.

Chapter Two

There Must Be a Law

▶ Breaks, Seats, Restrooms
▶ Sundays, Holidays, Rest Days
▶ Military Leave
▶ Health Insurance
▶ Smoking
▶ Closings and Layoffs
▶ Pensions
▶ Whistleblowers
▶ At-will Employment
▶ Child Labor

This chapter answers a number of frequently raised questions such as: Do employers have to provide breaks? Does overtime have to be paid on Sundays? Can a worker be fired without a reason?

BREAKS, SEATS, RESTROOMS

Employee working conditions are the subject of several state and federal labor laws.

Meal breaks. Massachusetts law mandates that employees who work more than six hours in a calendar day be given a break of at least thirty minutes for a meal.[56] The break may be unpaid, unless the employee is given responsibilities or is required to remain on the premises.[57] Providing two 15-minute breaks is not an equivalent. The law carries a fine of $300 to $600 and is enforced by the attorney general's Fair Labor Division.

Some schedules require two 30-minute breaks. To illustrate: A worker who begins the day at 8:00 A.M., eats lunch between 11:30 A.M. and noon, and works to 7:00 P.M. must be offered a second meal break at or before 6:00 P.M.

The law does not apply to the iron, glass, print, bleach, dye, paper, and letterpress industries. The attorney general can grant waivers to other factories, workshops, or mechanical establishments, but rarely does.[58]

Employers may not punish employees who complain about meal break violations or report to the attorney general. Discharged workers can sue for triple back pay.[59]

NOTE: An employer is not guilty of a violation if an employee, without being coerced, works through a meal period and is paid for the time.

Rest breaks. Massachusetts does not require employers to provide rest breaks. Compare this to California, Colorado, Kentucky, Nevada, Oregon, and Washington, where employers must allow ten minutes time off every four hours.

Seats

Employees must be allowed to sit during their work.[60] An exception applies if work cannot be performed properly or if sitting creates an unsafe condition. Employers must furnish suitable seating.

Lockers

Manufacturers, mercantile establishments, hotels, and railroads must provide lockers or other receptacles for employees who need to change clothes at work. Locks and keys must be supplied.[61]

Restrooms

Toilet facilities must be furnished by gender except for one-person restrooms that can be locked from the inside. The table below shows the number of amenities required.[62]

Number of Employees	Minimum Number of water closets for each gender
1-15	1
16-35	2
36-55	3
56-80	4
81-110	5
111-150	6
over 150	One additional toilet for each additional 40 employees

When toilet facilities are not being used by women, urinals can replace water closets as long as two-thirds of the minimum number of closets are furnished.

Construction sites are subject to the following requirements:

Number of Employees	Minimum Number
20 or fewer	1 toilet
20 or more	1 toilet and 1 urinal per 40 workers
200 or more	1 toilet and 1 urinal per 50 workers[63]

Restroom access. Workers must be allowed prompt access to toilet facilities. Employers may not impose rules or policies that cause extended delays.[64]

Washing facilities. Lavatories must be furnished with hot and cold running water, soap, and towels.

Heat

Workplaces must be heated from October 15 to May 15.[65] Guidelines are shown in the next table.

Workplace	Proper Heating (Fahrenheit)
Foundries	50 - 60
Factories	60 - 62
Machine shops	60 - 62
Public buildings	60 - 68
Restaurants	62 - 66
Warehouses	62 - 65
Theaters	62 - 65
Stores	65
Offices	66 - 68
Schools	66 - 68

First Aid

Employers must employ a person trained in first aid unless the workplace is near a hospital, clinic, or infirmary.[66]

Drinking Water

Industrial establishments and construction sites must furnish employees with fresh and pure drinking water.[67]

SUNDAYS, HOLIDAYS, REST DAYS

Sundays and holidays are a source of many controversies. Can businesses stay open? Do employees have to work? Must employers pay extra wages?

Sundays

Businesses that do not fall within a statutory exemption must obtain permission from the local chief of police to operate on Sundays.[68] Single-day permits can be granted to avoid serious suffering, loss, damage, public inconvenience, or a delay to military defense work.

Retail stores. Retail stores with eight or more employees cannot require nonexempt employees to work on Sundays.[69] Those who work must be paid time-and-one-half wages—even if their hours for the week do not exceed forty.[70]

Holidays

Massachusetts recognizes eleven legal holidays (see chart below). Holidays that fall on Sundays are observed on Mondays.

Seven days (see chart) are "Sunday Law" holidays, meaning that permits are necessary for manufacturers and other nonexempt enterprises to operate. Holiday criteria are the same as for Sundays with one difference: a police chief may grant a holiday permit to avoid serious production inconvenience.

Time off. Manufacturers cannot require employees to work on holidays unless the work is "absolutely necessary."[71]

Retail stores cannot require employees to work on New Year's Day, Memorial Day, Independence Day, Labor Day, Columbus Day after noon, or Veterans' Day after 1:00 P.M.[72]

Legal Holidays

New Year's Day	Bunker Hill Day
Martin Luther King Jr. Day	(Suffolk County only)
Presidents' Day	Independence Day*
Evacuation Day	Labor Day*
(Suffolk County only)	Columbus Day**
Patriots' Day	Veterans Day***
Memorial Day*	Thanksgiving *
	Christmas *

---

*, **, or *** Sunday Law Holiday
**Permit required to operate before noon
***Permit required to operate before 1 P.M.

Holiday pay. Other than retail stores, employers need not pay premium wages on holidays unless required by company policy or union contract. Retail establishments must pay time-and-one-half to nonexempt employees on New Year's Day, Memorial Day, Independence Day, Labor Day, Columbus Day after noon, and Veterans' Day after 1:00 P.M.[73]

Rest Days

Manufacturing, mechanical, and mercantile establishments (including retail stores and restaurants) may not require employees to work more than six continuous days.[74] Commercial, industrial, transportation, and communications enterprises that schedule employees to work on Sundays must allow at least one full day off during the next six days.[75] Employees can work seven days in a row on a voluntary basis.

The day-of-rest laws do not apply in the gas, electricity, milk, water, food (not including restaurants), rail, hotel, and newspaper industries. Nor are they applicable to janitors, drug store pharmacists, bakers, persons who care for machinery or animals, persons employed in farm or personal services, or persons who perform emergency services.[76]

Holy Days

Employees whose religious beliefs prohibit working may take time off on holy and Sabbath days.[77] Ten or more days of advance notice must be given (sample letter below). Requests may be denied if the absence will cause the employer "undue hardship."

September 1, 2008
Mark Sanders, Shift Supervisor

Dear Mr. Sanders:

This is to notify you that I will need the day off on October 9, 2008 to observe the Jewish high holy day of Yom Kippur. Please confirm that my request is approved.

Yours truly,
Steven Morris

The Massachusetts Commission Against Discrimination (MCAD) enforces the holy day law.

MILITARY LEAVE

Workers who perform military service, including service in the national guard and reserves, have job rights under the Uniformed Services Employment and Reemployment Rights Act (USERRA).[78] USERRA applies to public and private employers regardless of size. Notices of USERRA rights and benefits must be posted.

Reinstatement

USERRA requires employers to reemploy returning service members. The employee must give notice of leaving, serve no more than five years, be released with a satisfactory discharge, and report back to work in a timely fashion. The five-year period is extended in certain circumstances, such as when service is involuntarily prolonged. Employees must be reinstated to the positions and pay rates they would have attained had they remained on the job, or to comparable positions with the same pay and status.[79] If an employee is unable to perform a previous job, the employer must make a reasonable effort to find a suitable position. If necessary, the employee must be given refresher training. Employees who serve for more than 180 days may not be discharged except for cause for twelve months after their return. Employees who serve 31 to 180 days are protected for six months. Time served in the military must be added to pre- and post-service employment when determining vacations, job assignments, pensions, pay, and other benefits. Employees who serve frequently have USERRA rights on each occasion.

USERRA complaints can be filed with the Veterans' Employment and Training Service (VETS), a division of the U.S. Department of Labor. Civil suits may also be filed.

HEALTH INSURANCE

Several laws regulate health insurance in the workplace.

Universal Health Insurance

Legislation enacted in 2006 requires Massachusetts residents to purchase health insurance if an affordable plan is available. Employers with eleven or more full-time-equivalent employees must allow full-time employees to buy medical insurance with pretax dollars and must make fair and reasonable contributions to the costs of medical plans.[80]

Employers can meet the requirement for fair and reasonable contributions if they pay one-third or more of employees' individual premiums or if 25 percent of full-time employees buy company-subsidized insurance.[81] Employers which do not contribute must pay assessments, currently $295 per full-time employee, to a state free-care fund.

Insurers are prohibited from offering health plans that discriminate against low-income workers in regard to contributions. Employers may not pay smaller percentages for lower paid employees than for those who are more highly paid. An exception applies if the lower or higher rates are restricted to employees covered by collective bargaining agreements.[82] Employers may not penalize employees who draw on free care.

Continuation Coverage

A federal law known as COBRA allows workers, spouses, and dependents to stay in group health plans for up to eighteen months following a layoff, discharge, resignation, reduction of hours, strike, death, divorce, or the employer's bankruptcy.[83] The employee or beneficiary must pay the entire premium plus up to 2 percent for administration. COBRA applies to businesses with twenty or more employees. A similar state law applies to workplaces with two to nineteen employees.[84]

> **NOTE:** For the first thirty-one days after an employee ceases to be a member of an insurance group other than an HMO, the employer must continue to pay its share of the premium.[85]

Divorce. Employer-sponsored health plans must continue to cover spouses, at no additional cost, if a participant undergoes a divorce or legal separation.[86] Eligibility ends if either party remarries.

FMLA leave. Under the Family and Medical Leave Act (see Chapter 4), if a worker takes a qualifying leave of up to twelve weeks, the employer must pay for health coverage on the same terms that applied before the leave commenced.

SMOKING

State legislation adopted in 2004 prohibits smoking in enclosed workplaces including factories, offices, restaurants, and stores.[87] Smoking rooms are not allowed, even if ventilated. Outside smoking areas must be far enough away that smoke cannot enter the workplace. No smoking signs must be conspicuously posted.

The Massachusetts Department of Public Health (DPH) and local boards of health enforce the law. Employers can be fined $100 for each violation. Employees, customers, contractors, and visitors can also be fined. Employees may not be punished for reporting violations.

CLOSINGS AND LAYOFFS

Companies of a certain size that close facilities or institute large layoffs must provide employees with advance notice or pay up to sixty days of severance wages.

Advance Notice

The Worker Adjustment and Retraining Notification Act (WARN) applies to private sector employers with one hundred or more full-time workers.[88] Covered employers must provide at least sixty calendar days written notice to unions and affected employees before instituting:

- A closing that affects 50 or more full-time employees at a single site during a 30-day period
- A layoff of 50 to 499 full-time employees at a single site for six months or longer—if this represents one-third or more of the workforce and occurs during a 30-day period
- A layoff of 500 or more full-time employees at a single site for six months or longer

Contents. Notices to unions must state whether the entire plant will be closed, whether the closing or layoff is permanent, the expected date of the first termination, the anticipated schedule for further terminations, and the names and titles of affected employees.

Notices to unrepresented workers must explain when the employee will be terminated, whether bumping rights apply, and whether the action is permanent.

Exceptions. Employers do not have to furnish 60-day notices if a closing is due to a natural disaster or an unforeseeable circumstance, or if the notice would damage an attempt to save the business. In such cases the employer must give as much notice as is practicable. Notice is not required at the completion of a project if employees were told upon hiring that their employment was limited.

Health Insurance

Employers of fifty or more employees that institute full or partial plant closings must continue payments for ninety days to commercial, Blue Cross Blue Shield, and HMO group health insurance plans.[89] Employees must continue to pay their portions of the premium.

PENSIONS

A federal law called ERISA regulates private sector pension plans.[90]

Participation

Pension plans are not required. However, plans that are established must allow employees to participate if they are 21 years of age and have completed one year of service. Plans that vest benefits immediately—other than 401(k) plans—can require two years of service.

Vesting

Vesting refers to the point in time when an employee has a guaranteed right to benefits derived from employer pension contributions. ERISA allows plans to apply the following schedules:
- 100 percent vesting after five years (*cliff vesting*)
- 20 percent vesting after three years, 40 percent after four years, 60 percent after five years, 80 percent after six years, and 100 percent after seven years (*graded vesting*)

A vested employee who leaves employment for any reason retains his or her right to accrued benefits.

> **EXAMPLE:** Phil Marks has worked for six years for Nesmith Resistors, which has a cliff-vesting pension plan. If he takes a job with another company, he will remain qualified for a pension from Nesmith when he reaches retirement age.

It is illegal to dismiss an employee to avoid vesting.

Prudence

Pension plans must invest prudently. They may not loan funds to plan employers, administrators, or trustees. Participants may sue trustees or managers who mismanage plan assets.

Insurance

Defined benefit pension plans, plans that pay a specified monthly or yearly benefit, must buy insurance from the Pension Benefit Guaranty Corporation (PBGC), a federal agency. If a plan terminates without sufficient funds, PBGC takes over payments.

WHISTLEBLOWERS

Employees who observe supervisors or managers taking part in fraud, tax evasion, pollution, safety violations, price-fixing, or other misconduct may consider making reports to upper-level management or to law enforcement agencies. A danger, of course, is retaliation.

Health Care

One industry in which whistleblowing is protected is health care. A Massachusetts law prohibits health care facilities from punishing medical providers who disclose or threaten to disclose a practice that violates a law, regulation, or professional standard and endangers public health.[91] Providers can refuse to participate in illegal activities. Providers who complain about unsafe care are also protected.

Before reporting an activity to a public body, the provider must give written notice and a reasonable opportunity for the facility to make corrections. Exceptions apply if the situation is an emergency, if the employee fears physical harm, or if the provider is reporting a crime.

Whistleblowers who are discharged or otherwise retaliated against can sue for reinstatement, damages, and legal fees.

Health care facilities must post notices that inform employees of their rights and list the names of managers designated to receive whistleblower notifications.

Corporate Fraud

The Sarbanes-Oxley Act of 2002 (SOX) applies to companies whose stock is sold on a public market.[92] It forbids punishment for reporting violations of federal securities or accountancy laws or activities involving stockholder fraud. Examples include overpaying invoices or doing business with contractors because of personal relationships.

An employee who is discriminated against because of a SOX report must file a complaint with the Occupational Safety and Health Administration (OSHA) within 90 days.

Environmental and Safety Violations

Several laws shield employees who report environmental or safety malfeasance. These include the Asbestos Hazard Emergency Response Act, the International Safety Container Act, the Safe Drinking Water Act, the Toxic Substances Control Act, the Solid Waste Disposal Act, the Federal Water Pollution Control Act, the Clean Air Act, the Superfund Act, the Energy Reorganization Act, the Pipeline Safety Improvement Act, the Wendell H. Ford Aviation Act (AIR 21), the Surface Transportation Assistance Act, and the Occupational Safety and Health Act. Protected activities include objecting to supervisors, refusing illegal orders, and notifying law enforcement.

Retaliation complaints must be filed with the Occupational Safety and Health Administration (OSHA).[93] The deadline is 30 days except for complaints under the International Safety Container Act (60 days), the Asbestos Hazard Act (90 days), AIR 21 (90 days), the Surface Transportation Assistance Act (180 days), the Pipeline Safety Improvement Act (180 days), and the Energy Reorganization Act (180 days).

Government Employees

A Massachusetts law protects state and local government employees who report misconduct to supervisors, managers, or public bodies.[94] The report must concern the violation of a law, rule, or regulation or a risk to public health, safety, or the environment. Employees can refuse to take part in the activity.

Before taking the matter to an outside body, the employee must give written notice and afford the agency a reasonable amount of time to make corrections. Exceptions apply if the situation is an emergency, if the employee reasonably fears physical harm, or if the employee is reporting a crime. Employees punished for whistleblowing can sue for triple damages.

EXAMPLE: A jury ordered the Commonwealth to pay $1.15 million to a state trooper who was punished by his superiors for reporting illegal wiretapping.

Government Contracts

Federal and state *qui tam* laws allow employees to sue contractors which engage in government contract fraud.[95] Employees can cite practices such as overbilling, substandard work, or exaggerated results. If the government takes over the suit, a qui tam plaintiff can be awarded 15 to 25 percent of the proceeds. If the government fails to join, a court can award the plaintiff up to 30 percent. Since potential judgments are three times the contract, a qui tam plaintiff can reap a substantial reward.

EXAMPLE: Sylvia Pecco worked for a firm holding a three-year $12 million research contract with the U.S. Department of Defense. At the end of the first year, the firm exaggerated test results to keep the contract. Aware of the fraud, Pecco sued in federal court. The government took over and recovered $36 million, of which $9 million was awarded to Pecco.

AT-WILL EMPLOYMENT

Workers without union or individual contracts are known as *at-will employees*. As a general rule, an employer can change an at-will employee's duties, reduce his or her salary, or discontinue employment "for any reason or for no reason at all."[96] Only a few exceptions are recognized.

Predatory Discharge

One type of discharge for which an at-will employee can take legal action is a firing whose underlying purpose is to save the employer from paying earned bonuses or commissions. Victims of predatory discharges can sue for damages.[97]

Public Policy Discharge

At-will employees can also sue if they are terminated for conduct that is statutorally protected or mandated. Examples include refusing to commit an unlawful act, asserting a legally guaranteed right, or reporting criminal wrongdoing.[98]

Malicious Discharge

In some circumstances, an at-will employee can sue for "malicious" interference with employment. An example is a termination for spiteful purposes.[99]

CHILD LABOR

Child labor laws regulate the hours and occupations of employees under the age of 18. Employers can be fined up to $11,000 for a violation, even if the minor is working for a family enterprise. Employers must post daily schedules, including mealtimes, at the beginning of each workweek.[100]

The table below summarizes current standards. Contact the Massachusetts Fair Labor Division or the U.S. Department of Labor to report violations.

Hours and Jobs That Minors May Work (other than on farms)

Age	Hours of Work	Permitted Occupations
9-11	Not during school hours Not after 8 P.M. or before 6 A.M.	Newspaper sales or delivery (written permission from parent or guardian required)
12-13	Same as above	Newspaper sales and delivery Street trades (sales, shoe shining) Limited seasonal work with permission from the U.S. Secretary of Labor Limited entertainment work Badge needed from the superintendent of schools

---

Age	Hours of Work	Permitted Occupations
14-15	Not during school hours except in approved work-experience and career-exploration programs Not before 7 A.M. or after 7 P.M. except during the summer (June 1 through Labor Day) when evening hours are extended to 9 P.M. Not more than three hours in any one day when school is in session Not more than eighteen hours per school week except in approved work experience and career exploration programs in which case not more than twenty-three hours Not more than forty hours per week when school is not in session Not more than eight hours a day when school is not in session Not more than six days per week	Non-hazardous occupations such as office, sales, clerical, food-serving (limited cooking and no baking), gas station (non-mechanical), supermarket bagging, cashiering, and lawn-care (but no power mowers) No jobs in warehouses, construction, communications, public utilities or transportation or in occupations prohibited for 16 and 17 year olds Call state or federal agencies for legality of particular jobs (state: 617-727-3465; federal: 617-624-6700) Work permit needed from superintendent of schools
16-17	Not before 6 A.M. or after 10 P.M. on nights preceding a regularly scheduled school day (10:15 P.M. in establishments that stop serving customers at 10 P.M.). Not before 6 A.M. or after 11:30 P.M. on nights not preceding a regularly scheduled school day (exceptions: restaurants and race tracks where work can continue until midnight) Not after 8 P.M. without direct and immediate adult supervision (exceptions: carts or kiosks in enclosed shopping malls with security until closing) Not more than six days per week Not more than nine hours per day[101] Not more than forty-eight hours per week	Occupations not classified as hazardous (for example, jobs which do not require the operation of certain power-driven machinery or extensive driving) No handling of alcohol or explosives Work permit needed from superintendent of schools

Questions *and* Answers

ON THE SPOT

Q. I was fired at 4:55 P.M. on a Friday afternoon. Wasn't I entitled to more than five minutes notice?

A. No. Employers can terminate employees without advance notice.

WITNESS SUBPOENA

Q. I have been subpoenaed to testify in a criminal trial. Can my employer punish me for missing work?

A. No. It is illegal to penalize an employee who is subpoenaed to testify in a criminal trial.[102]

JURY DUTY

Q. My boss says he will terminate me if I serve as a juror. Can he do this?

A. No. Employers may not discharge, coerce, discriminate against, or harass employees who serve on juries.[103] Nor may an employer interfere with a juror's effectiveness, attentiveness, or peace of mind.

NON-COMPETE AGREEMENT

Q. On my first day of work, I signed an agreement that if I should resign I would not work for a company in the same industry. Is the agreement binding?

A. Perhaps. Non-compete agreements are valid in Massachusetts— except for physicians, nurses, attorneys, and broadcast employees— if they protect legitimate business interests, are not unreasonably long, and do not cover an overly large geographical area.

FEDERAL WORKERS

Q. Do the state laws discussed in this chapter apply to federal employees?

A. No. Generally speaking, states do not have jurisdiction over federal agencies except in areas such as unemployment insurance, where Congress has chosen to defer to local authority.

POSTERS

Q. What labor law posters must be displayed at the workplace?

A. The following, with the agency supplying the poster in parentheses:

- Safety and health (OSHA)
- Federal minimum wage, overtime, equal pay, child labor (DOL)
- State minimum wage (attorney general)
- Equal employment opportunity (EEOC)
- Fair employment (MCAD)
- Family and medical leave (DOL)
- Federal contractors (OFCCP)
- Maternity leave (MCAD)
- Lie detector tests (DOL)
- Unemployment insurance (DUA)
- Davis-Bacon Act (DOL)
- Walsh-Healey and Service Contract Acts (DOL)
- USERRA (DOL)
- Whistleblower protections
- No smoking
- Day of rest
- Hours of minors

thoughts for change

DID YOU SAY MONTANA?

Montana is the only state that has abolished employment at will. The state's Wrongful Discharge Act prohibits discharges without good cause and allows workers to sue. The law does not appear to have hindered the state's economic growth.

Chapter Three
Personal Rights

▶ Inquiries and Examinations
▶ Tests
▶ Searches, Detention, Eavesdropping
▶ Personnel Records
▶ Complaints and Protests

This chapter discusses issues related to personal rights, including the right to privacy, the right not to be unreasonably searched or tested, the right to examine one's personnel file, and the right to complain about working conditions.

INQUIRIES AND EXAMINATIONS

Employers are prohibited from addressing certain questions to job applicants or current employees. Medical examinations are also regulated.

Criminal Record

The Massachusetts Fair Employment Practices Act (FEPA), which covers employers with six or more workers, prohibits questions that could make a job applicant or employee reveal:

- An arrest that did not result in a conviction
- A first conviction for drunkenness, simple assault, affray, speeding, minor traffic violations, or disturbing the peace
- A misdemeanor conviction more than 5 years old, unless the person has been convicted of another offense in the past 5 years[104]

The following inquiries violate the law: "Do you have a criminal record?" "Have you ever been arrested?" "Have you ever been convicted?" Employers may not reject or dismiss employees for refusing to answer illegal questions or for answering untruthfully.[105]

Job applications may ask about felony convictions or misdemeanors not listed in FEPA. The following notice is required:

An applicant for employment with a sealed record on file with the commissioner of probation may answer 'no record' with respect to an inquiry herein relative to prior arrests, criminal court appearances or convictions. In addition, any applicant for employment may answer 'no record' with respect to any inquiry relative to prior arrests, court appearances and adjudications in all cases of delinquency or as a child in need of services which did not result in a complaint transferred to the superior court for criminal prosecution.[106]

CORI. Despite FEPA, the Massachusetts Criminal Offender Record Information Act, known as CORI, allows employers to obtain adult conviction and pending case data from the Criminal History Systems Board (CHSB).[107] Information is supplied if a job applicant or employee has been convicted of a crime punishable by five years imprisonment or more or has recently been incarcerated or on probation. Employers certified by the CHSB as having a "public interest" in offender information can access more extensive data.

Some employers are required by law to obtain CORI records. For example, public and private schools must conduct checks at least once every three years for employees having contact with children.[108]

Disability Inquiries

FEPA also forbids employers from questioning job applicants (including applicants for transfers or promotions) about disabilities or requiring medical examinations, unless the employer first extends a conditional job offer.[109] A conditional job offer is an offer whose sole qualification is that the applicant pass a medical review. Agility and drug tests are generally not classified as medical examinations.

Specific inquiries. According to the Massachusetts Commission Against Discrimination (MCAD), the following pre-job-offer questions are illegal:

"Have you ever received workers' compensation?"

"Do you have a handicap or disability?"

"Have you been treated for any of the following conditions?"

"Have you been rejected for health or life insurance?"

"Have you been hospitalized for a medical or mental condition?"

"Do you have AIDS?"

"Do you have any handicaps or limitations that would prevent you from doing the job?"

"Have you ever been absent from work due to an illness or an injury?"

"Have you ever received psychiatric treatment?"

"Do you have a physical handicap, disease, or other disability which should be considered in assigning you to work?"

"Have you ever been addicted to illegal drugs or treated for drug abuse or alcoholism?"[110]

Genetic information. Employers may not ask applicants or employees about their genetic backgrounds.[111]

Current employees. Current employees may not be required to undergo medical or psychiatric examinations unless there is a business necessity for the review.[112] An example is an employee who is unable to perform a job duty.[113] Necessity may also present itself if the employee's condition poses a threat to himself or to others, or if a law or regulation requires periodic physicals.[114]

NOTE: Medical information obtained from employees must be kept in confidential files. Records may only be revealed to managers who need to know about restrictions and accommodations, first aid and safety personnel (if a disability could require emergency treatment), government investigators, workers' compensation insurers, and benefit plan insurers.[115]

TESTS

To what extent may employers conduct drug, HIV, or lie detector tests?

Drug Tests

Unlike in some states, no Massachusetts statute expressly regulates when employers can or cannot test for drugs. Nonetheless, judges sometimes imply restrictions from the state privacy act or the state or federal constitution.

Massachusetts Privacy Act. Employers can generally test employees whose behavior is erratic or who commit misconduct. Random testing is a different matter. The Massachusetts Privacy Act bars unreasonable interference with personal privacy.[116] In a lead case the Supreme Judicial Court barred a company from urine testing a technical editor on a random basis. In the same decision, however, it approved testing of an account executive who drove company vehicles 20,000 miles per year.[117]

Government employees. Public sector employees can challenge drug testing under Article 14 of the Massachusetts Constitution which forbids governmental authorities from conducting unreasonable searches and seizures. In a Boston case, the Supreme Judicial Court ruled that random urine testing of police officers violated Article 14 in the absence of evidence of widespread drug use.[118] The decision does not prohibit testing for cause, such as when an officer violates a policy or causes an accident. Nor does it restrict hair sample testing.

Mandated testing. Federal rules require transport carriers to conduct random and post-accident drug and alcohol testing of safety-sensitive employees.[119] Similar rules apply to the nuclear industry.

HIV Tests

It is illegal to ask a job applicant or employee to undergo an HIV test.[120]

Genetic Tests

Employers may not solicit, require, or administer genetic tests as a condition of employment.[121] Nor may genetic information, including family histories, be considered in making hiring, firing, or promotion decisions.

Lie Detector Tests

Employers may not ask employees or job seekers to undergo lie detector tests.[122] An exception applies if the test is administered by a law enforcement agency. Lie detector tests include traditional polygraph examinations as well as other tests that measure honesty or trustworthiness.

SEARCHES, DETENTION, EAVESDROPPING

To what extent may employers search, detain, or spy on employees?

Searches

An employer that has a legitimate suspicion that a worker's locker or desk contains stolen goods or other contraband can conduct a search. Employers can also examine computers for offensive content, at least where they have pre-informed employees of the possibility. Searches must be handled with discretion. If supervisors or guards humiliate an innocent employee in front of coworkers, the employee may be able to sue for defamation of character.

Employers may take reasonable security measures to prevent theft, including inspecting bags as employees leave. Employees may not be singled out by race, nationality, or sex.

Video monitoring is lawful other than in bathrooms, locker rooms, or private offices where employees have a reasonable expectation of privacy.

Detention

Employees suspected of criminal activity or other misconduct can be ordered to remain on the premises while the police are called or the employer conducts an investigation.[123] Force may not be used or threatened.

Eavesdropping

State law forbids the use of electronic or mechanical devices to eavesdrop on conversations.[124] Employers may not secretly record conversations with employees, place recorders in work or rest areas, or intercept telephone calls. The statute does not apply to backing up and retrieving email conversations.

Illegal eavesdropping carries a fine of up to $10,000 and a prison sentence of up to five years. An employee whose firing is based on illegally obtained information can sue for back pay, emotional distress, and punitive damages.

PERSONNEL RECORDS

The Massachusetts Personnel Records Act (MPRA) affords current and former employees employees the right to review their personnel records within five days of a written request.[125] The employee does not need to state a reason. Copies must furnished within five days if requested.[126] Employers of twenty or more workers must retain personnel records from the date employment begins until three years after employment ends. The law is enforced by the Attorney General's Fair Labor Division. Violators are subject to fines of $500 to $2,500.

The MPRA defines a personnel record as any record that refers to an employee by name and has been used for or may affect discipline or the employee's qualifications for hiring, promotion, transfer, or compensation. Job applications, credit checks, letters of reference, test results, performance evaluations, warnings, supervisor's notes, attendance records, witness statements, and medical histories clearly fall within this definition—whether or not they are kept in the employee's main personnel file. Employers can withhold records that contain personal information about others.

Employees can invoke their rights to prepare for a grievance meeting, to investigate a possible lawsuit, to prepare a job application, or simply to learn the content of a file.

An employee who disagrees with material in his or her file can ask for its removal. If the employer refuses, the employee must be allowed to insert a letter refuting the information. Union employees can grieve to expunge false information. Nonunion employees can sue.

The MPRA does not apply to tenured or tenure-track instructors at private colleges and universities.

REQUEST TO REVIEW RECORDS

April 1, 2008

Louise Wayland
Director of Human Relations
Newton Hospital
10 Forbes Rd.
Newton, MA 02116

Dear Ms. Wayland:

I request permission to review my personnel records covering September 1, 1999 to the present. This includes, but is not limited to, disciplinary records, performance evaluations, salary reviews, and all other documents that identify me and could affect my employment, whether or not included in my regular file.

Please notify me when I can perform my review.

Thank you for your attention to this matter.

Yours truly,

Helen Martell

COMPLAINTS AND PROTESTS

Griping about pay, conditions, and supervision is inherent in being an employee. Nonetheless, bosses sometimes consider it grounds for discipline. It is not widely known, but labor law protects employees who collectively complain or protest about working conditions—even if the employees are nonunion.

Concerted activity. The National Labor Relations Act (NLRA) guarantees private sector employees the right to take part in concerted activities for their mutual aid or protection.[127] The law is enforced by the National Labor Relations Board (NLRB). Concerted activity includes two or more employees acting together, one worker acting for a group, or one worker trying to induce group action. Complaining to coworkers, customers, supervisors, and even the press is protected if two or more employees take part or if the goal is to spur a collective response.

EXAMPLE: Lawrence Leinweber, a nonunion engineer, sent mail to several co-employees complaining that a new company vacation policy would result in fewer days off. The next day he was terminated. The NLRB said his actions were concerted and ordered him reinstated with back pay.[128]

Concerted activity is protected even if employees use disrespectful language. In one case, an employee told another that a boss was "prejudiced." In another case, a worker referred to a chief executive as a "cheap son of a bitch." The NLRB said that both employees were protected against retaliation.[129]

Illegal rules. Work rules, codes of conduct, or handbooks that discourage or inhibit group action can violate the law even if the employer does not issue warnings or discipline.[130] The following are examples of directives that have been ruled unlawful:

- "Employees may not solicit other employees or distribute literature on company premises."[131]
- "Employees may not fraternize with other employees."
- "Employees may not disclose or discuss another employee's compensation without that employee's permission."
- "Employees may not reveal sensitive information concerning the company to any nonemployee."
- "Employees may not engage in activities that interfere with operations or production."
- "Employees who walk off the job will be discharged."

Protests. Both union and nonunion employees have a right to wear protest buttons, distribute handbills, submit petitions, organize letter-writing campaigns, picket, or even refuse to work — as long as the protest concerns a job matter, does not use obscene language, and does not attack the quality of the employer's goods or services.[132] Workers can form caucuses or committees to advance their demands.

Employees whose rights to protest or organize are interfered with can file unfair labor practice charges with the National Labor Relations Board (NLRB) (see address on page 155). Charge forms can be filled out on the NLRB website.

Questions *and* Answers

Long hair

Q: My company forbids beards and long hair. Don't I have a right to decide my own appearance?

A: Not at work. No law prevents employers from imposing grooming standards.

Patronage

Q: I hold a supervisory position in the city parks department. If a Republican wins the next mayor's election, could he fire me because I belong to the Democrats?

A: No. In the public sector, the only employees who can be dismissed because of political affiliation are high-level policymakers and persons providing confidential services to policymakers, such as personal secretaries or speechwriters.

Religious principles

Q: I work for an advertising agency. One of our customers is a weapons manufacturer. My religion is opposed to all forms of militarism. Can I insist on not working on the account?

A: Perhaps. An employer must accommodate an employee's religious beliefs and practices, including making changes in assignments, unless the accommodation will cause the employer to suffer undue hardship.[133]

Detective agency

Q: Can an employer hire a detective agency to surveil employees suspected of sick leave fraud?

A: Yes. The Fair Credit Reporting Act used to prohibit employers from hiring outside professionals to secretly investigate employees. In 2003, however, after a business lobbying campaign, Congress deleted the restriction.[134]

Meddling

Q: A case manager in my department is upset because I was promoted ahead of him. He is threatening to reveal embarrassing information about my private life. If he gets me fired, could I sue him?

A: Perhaps. An employee can sue a coworker who maliciously and without justifiable cause induces the employer to discharge the employee.[135]

Dating

Q: Can a company policy prohibit employees from dating each other?

A: Yes.

Smoking

Q: Can a business refuse to hire employees who smoke?

A: Yes. Unlike thirty states, Massachusetts does not protect smokers from discriminatory treatment.[136]

Confidentiality

Q: I asked my boss for time off to obtain psychiatric treatment. Can she tell others about my condition?

A: Usually not. Employers must keep medical information confidential unless it is needed by a supervisor or manager to determine restrictions or accommodations, or by first aid or safety personnel to provide emergency treatment.

Political activities

Q: Can an at-will employee be fired because she is a member of a left-wing organization or because she attends a political rally?

A: Yes. Unlike states such as Connecticut (see below) Massachusetts does not ban discrimination against private sector employees based on political association or expression.[137]

t h o u g h t s   f o r   c h a n g e

DOES THE NUTMEG STATE HAVE THE RIGHT IDEA?

Connecticut extends free speech rights to employees in the private sector through the following law:

> Any employer ... who subjects any employee to discipline or discharge on account of the exercise ... of rights guaranteed by the first amendment to the United States Constitution ... provided that such activity does not substantially or materially interfere with the employee's bona fide job performance or the working relationship between the employee and the employer, shall be liable to such employee for damages ... including punitive damages ...[138]

Chapter Four

Medical and Family Leave

▶ Family and Medical Leave
▶ Small Necessities Leave
▶ Maternity Leave

For years, the only law guaranteeing time off from work was a state maternity leave statute. The Family and Medical Leave Act (FMLA), passed by Congress in 1993, considerably expanded worker rights.[139] The Massachusetts Small Necessities Leave Act (SNLA), enacted in 1998, added further protections.[140]

FAMILY AND MEDICAL LEAVE

The FMLA allows eligible employees to take up to twelve weeks leave over twelve months.

In Brief
Family and Medical Leave Act

COVERED EMPLOYERS
- Private sector employers with fifty or more employees
- Public agencies

MAJOR PROVISIONS
- Eligible employees may take time off from work (leave) for up to twelve weeks a year:
  - If unable to work due to a serious health condition
  - To care for family members with serious health conditions
  - For childbirth or to bond with newborn, adopted, or foster children
- Military families have additional rights (see page 74).

ENFORCEMENT AGENCY
- Wage and Hour Division of the U.S. Department of Labor (see page 156)

PENALTIES
An employer may be ordered to:
- Allow time off
- Provide reinstatement and back pay to employees discharged or refused reinstatement because of protected absences
- Promote an employee who has been denied advancement because of FMLA absences

ADDITIONAL INFORMATION
- Employers must continue medical insurance during FMLA leaves on the same basis as when employees were working.
- Employers may not penalize employees for taking FMLA time off.
- Employers must post notices explaining FMLA benefits.

Eligibility

An employee is eligible for FMLA time off if he or she:

1. Has worked for a covered employer for at least twelve months; and

2. Has worked at least 1,250 hours during the twelve months prior to the commencement of the leave; and

3. Works at a location where the employer employs fifty or more persons within a 75-mile radius.

Months served. The twelve months of employment need not be consecutive. For example, an employee who works for three months, resigns, is rehired four years later, and works for nine months, meets the standard.

Hours worked. The 1,250-hour requirement is time actually worked. Medical absences and vacations are not counted. The rule disqualifies persons who average fewer than 25 hours per week as well as those who lose substantial periods of time from work.

NOTE: Salaried employees are deemed to meet the 1,250-hour requirement unless the employer can prove otherwise.

Seventy-five miles. Surface miles over public roads determine the 75-mile radius within which fifty employees must work.

Leave Year

The 12-month period during which employees can take twelve weeks of leave is known as the FMLA leave year. Employers must choose among four options:

1. The calendar year

2. Another fixed period such as the employer's fiscal year or the employee's anniversary year

3. The 12-month period after an employee first takes FMLA leave

4. The 12-month period before each date an employee uses FMLA leave

Medical Leave

FMLA medical leave can be taken on a continuous, intermittent, or reduced-schedule basis. Employers may not impose penalties, refuse reinstatement, or take other adverse action because an employee misses work for an FMLA condition.

Serious health condition. To qualify for FMLA medical leave, an employee must be unable to work due to a serious health condition. Leave is not available for minor problems such as colds or upset stomachs. Under the FMLA regulations, a condition is serious if it involves:

- An overnight stay in a hospital
- A disability of more than three consecutive days that requires continuing treatment by a health care provider
- A chronic disorder
- Pregnancy
- A long term or permanent disorder
- Multiple treatments to prevent a period of incapacity of more than three consecutive days

Short-term condition. Temporary illnesses or injuries qualify as serious if they disable an employee for more than three consecutive days and require continuing medical treatment.

The consecutive requirement refers to calendar days. An employee who is disabled Friday, Saturday, Sunday, and Monday satisfies the criterion even if no work is scheduled on the weekend.

Two visits to a health care provider constitute continuing medical treatment, as well as one visit followed by a regimen of physical therapy, therapeutic devices, or prescription medications.

EXAMPLE: Phil Grady suffered a skin infection on Sunday. He saw a doctor and was given a 10-day prescription for antibiotics. He was unable to work Monday, Tuesday, and Wednesday. Because his absence meets the requirements for a serious health condition, his employer cannot count it under its attendance control program.

Reduced schedule. An employer must reduce an employee's schedule if an FMLA condition prevents the employee from working full-time. For example, an employee may only be able to work half-time after an operation. Employers must furnish reduced schedules even if company policy forbids part-time work. The time-lost percentage is multiplied by twelve to determine the number of weeks available.

Advance notice. Employees must give thirty days advance notice before taking a planned FMLA leave. An employee who has less than thirty days foreknowledge must give as much notice as is practicable. Advance notice is not required for absences that are unforeseeable.

Employees do not have to mention the FMLA when requesting leaves or reporting absences.[141] But they must provide enough information for the employer to understand that a serious health condition is involved. Calling in "sick" is not sufficient.

Certification. Employers can require medical certifications. The employee's health care provider must describe the condition, state that the employee is unable to work, and project the condition's duration. For intermittent leave, the provider should estimate the frequency of absences or state that leave will be needed on a sporadic basis.

Employers must allow fifteen days for certifications. If the report is inadequate or incomplete, the employer must allow additional time for the provider to correct the deficiency.[142]

After receiving a certification, an employer can ask an employee to submit to an examination by a second provider. The second provider may not be on the payroll or do regular business with the employer. If the second provider states that the employee is not disabled or is not suffering from a serious health condition, the employer can insist on an examination by a third provider chosen jointly by the employer and the employee. The third provider's opinion is binding.

Family-Care Leave

Family-care leave can be taken to care for family members with serious health conditions. Leave requests cannot be delayed or denied because the employee holds an important position, work is busy, or other relatives are available. The leave can be taken on a continuous, intermittent, or reduced-schedule basis.

EXAMPLE: Theresa Pyne's 9-year-old son suffers recurrent asthma attacks. Pyne works a 5-day schedule. She may take up to sixty FMLA days a year to care for her son.

Family members. The FMLA defines family members as children younger than 18, spouses, and parents. Leave can be taken for older sons or daughters if they are incapable of self-care because of physical or mental disabilities.[143] Leave may not be taken for grandparents or grandchildren.[144]

Care. Care includes cooking meals, driving family members to appointments, changing dressings, providing emotional support, and attending conferences with providers.

Travel. Employees may take leave to care for family members who live in other states or countries. Certifications from foreign providers must be accepted.

Childbirth, Adoption, and Foster Placement Leave

FMLA leave may be taken for childbirth, to care for a newborn child, or to bond with an adopted or foster child. Unlike absences for medical and family care, employers can insist that leaves be taken for a single continuous period.

Parents. Mothers and fathers may take childbirth or newborn-care leave when a baby is born or at any point before the child reaches the age of one. Adoption and foster-care leave may be taken up to one year after placement. Parents can take leave at the same time, consecutively, or at different times during the year

> **NOTE:** If both parents work for the same employer, the employer can impose a twelve-week maximum for time off for childbirth, newborn care, adoption, or foster placement.[145] For example, if the mother takes eight weeks, the father can be restricted to four weeks.

Pay

Employers do not have to pay wages during FMLA leaves unless the absence qualifies under a sick or disability program. Employees for whom such payments are unavailable must be allowed to draw on their accrued paid vacation or personal time.[146]

> **EXAMPLE:** Noreen Marks missed four days from work after her child contracted pneumonia. She has three weeks of accrued vacation. She may request four days of vacation pay.

Imposing paid leave. Employers can insist that employees use their accrued paid vacation and personal days during FMLA absences despite the employee's desire to save the days. An exception applies if substitution conflicts with a collective bargaining agreement; for example, if employees have the right to schedule vacations at times of their own choosing.[147]

Return to Work

When leaves are over, employees who are able to perform their duties must be restored to their original jobs or to equivalent positions. If a new position is assigned, it must satisfy three tests in reference to the original position:

1. Pay, benefits, working conditions, privileges, and status must be virtually identical.

2. Skills, efforts, responsibility, and authority must be substantially equivalent.

3. Duties must be substantially similar.

Employers may not assign returning employees to more distant work locations or to less desirable shifts. A union employee may not be assigned to a nonunion job.

Fitness report. An employee who takes a medical leave may be required to provide a fitness-for-duty report prior to returning. Employers may not insist on physical examinations unless this procedure is specified in a collective bargaining agreement or required by a federal or state law.[148]

Key employees. Salaried workers whose pay is among the highest ten percent in the workplace are considered key employees under the FMLA. Key employees cannot be denied the right to take leaves for FMLA purposes. They can, however, be denied reinstatement if this would cause the employer to suffer grievous economic harm.[149]

Enforcement

An employee who is refused time off, penalized, or fired because of an FMLA absence can file a complaint with the U.S. Department of Labor Wage and Hour Division or sue in court. The statute of limitations is two years unless the violation is willful, in which case the period is three years.

SMALL NECESSITIES LEAVE

The Massachusetts Small Necessities Leave Act (SNLA) allows FMLA-eligible employees up to twenty-four hours of unpaid time off every twelve months to:
* Participate in children's school activities
* Accompany children or elderly relatives to routine medical appointments
* Accompany elderly relatives to appointments for professional services

School Activities

School activities under the SNLA must directly relate to the "educational advancement" of a son or daughter.[150] Examples include parent-teacher conferences, special education meetings, and interviews for new schools. Chaperoning trips may also qualify. Schools include licensed day care facilities and head start programs, but not colleges or universities.

Children's Medical Appointments

Routine medical or dental appointments include checkups and camp examinations.[151]

Elderly Relatives

The SNLA defines elderly relatives as persons 60 years of age or older who are related by blood or marriage.[152] Parents, spouses, grandparents, uncles, aunts, siblings, and in-laws can qualify. The relative need not live in the employee's home.

Intermittent Leave

SNLA leave can be taken intermittently. For example, an employee who needs four hours for a parent-teacher conference, could take as many as six leaves in a year. Employees can be forced to use accrued vacation or personal time.

Notice

Employees must give at least seven days notice before using SNLA leave. If this is impossible, the employee must give notice as soon as is practicable. It is not necessary to refer to the law when requesting time off.

Certification

Employers can ask employees to certify their need for leave. The certification should state the date, duration, and purpose. See sample below. Additional information can be requested to verify that a leave qualifies.[153]

SNLA CERTIFICATION

I certify that on _____ (date) I will/did take _____ hours of leave for the following purpose:

____ to participate in school activities directly related to the educational advancement of my son or daughter.

____ to accompany my son or daughter to a routine medical or dental appointment.

____ to accompany an elderly relative to a routine medical or dental appointment or to an appointment for professional services related to the relative's care.

Signature _____

Date _____

Enforcement

Employees can file SNLA complaints with the attorney general's Fair Labor Division or sue in court.[154] In the event of a discharge, a court can order reinstatement, triple backpay, and reimbursement for legal expenses.

MATERNITY LEAVE

The Massachusetts Maternity Leave Act (MMLA) allows full-time employees to take eight weeks of unpaid leave before or after the birth or adoption of a child.[155] Though this is less time than the FMLA allows, the MMLA applies to employers with as few as six workers—far more employers than are covered by the FMLA. The MMLA is also valuable to employees who use up their FMLA weeks prior to childbirth. The law is enforced by the Massachusetts Commission Against Discrimination (MCAD).

Eligibility

To qualify for MMLA leave an employee must have completed her probationary period. If there is no such period, the employee must have worked full-time for three consecutive months. Employees must give at least two weeks notice and state their intentions to return.

Return to Work

Employees who take MMLA leave have a right to return to their original positions. If the post has been filled on a permanent basis, the employer must assign the employee to an equally paid position which has similar duties and working conditions. Reinstatement is not required if a layoff takes place during the leave which would have included the employee had she remained working, or if the employer eliminates the employee's position for reasons unrelated to her absence.

Questions *and* Answers

Whiplash

Q: I suffered whiplash in a car accident. Due to neck pain I missed one day from work the week of the accident, one day the next week, and two days the week after. Are my absences protected by the FMLA?

A: No. To qualify as a serious health condition, an illness or injury must cause more than three consecutive days of incapacity.

Modified duty

Q: I was approved for three weeks of leave to recover from an operation. Can my boss order me to come back on light duty?

A: No. Employers must permit FMLA-eligible employees to stay home from work until they can perform their regular duties.

NOTE: Take caution. Refusing a light-duty job offer may jeopardize any benefits you are receiving under workers' compensation or disability insurance.

Late arrival

Q: I was two hours late because of a migraine headache. Did this come under the FMLA?

A: Yes, if you have a chronic condition and gave proper notice.

Chickenpox

Q: Can I take FMLA leave for a child with chickenpox?

A: Probably not. Chickenpox rarely qualifies as a serious health condition.

Filling in

Q: My sister cares for my father, who has Alzheimer's disease. Can I use FMLA time to fill in for her during the summer?

A: Yes. FMLA leave can be taken to fill in for a regular caregiver.

Unmarried father

Q: My girlfriend is pregnant. Can I take an FMLA leave when the baby is born?

A: Yes. Parents do not have to be married to take newborn care leave.

Workers' compensation

Q: Our company counts workers' compensation time as FMLA. Legal?

A: Yes. Workers' compensation injuries usually meet the tests for serious health conditions—allowing employers to subtract the time from employee FMLA entitlements.

Half-time schedule

Q: After eight weeks on childbirth leave, I asked to come back half-time. Does my boss have to accommodate me?

A: No. Employers do not have to provide reduced schedules to employees who request time off for childbirth or newborn care purposes.

Medical appointment

Q: Can I take time off from work to see my doctor?

A: This depends. Absences to obtain treatments for serious health conditions can, with proper notice, qualify for FMLA leave.[156] Employers can insist, however, that employees attempt to schedule appointments outside work hours.[157]

Double time

Q: Can an employee who gives birth to twins take extra time off?

A: Yes. According to MCAD guidelines, mothers are entitled to eight weeks of leave for each newborn child.[158]

Military families

Q: What leave rights are available for military families?

A: In January, 2008, Congress amended the FMLA to allow twelve weeks of leave if a spouse, child, or parent serving in the armed forces in support of a "contingency" operation suffers a qualifying "exigency." In addition, leaves of up to twenty-six weeks must be allowed if an employee is needed to care for a family member who suffers a service-related injury. The Department of Labor is expected to issue regulations explaining the rules by the end of 2008.

Chapter Five

Safety and Health

▶ Safety Standards
▶ OSHA Complaints
▶ Duty to Provide Information
▶ Worker Rights

W orkplace health and safety is regulated by the Occupational Safety and Health Administration (OSHA), a federal agency created by the 1970 Occupational Safety and Health Act (OSH Act).[159]

OSHA standards apply to all industries except those regulated by other federal agencies, such as mining and trucking. State and local government workplaces are excluded. OSHA has offices in Methuen, Braintree, and Springfield.

In Brief
Occupational Safety and Health Act

COVERED EMPLOYERS
- Private sector employers
- U.S. Postal Service
- Federal agencies (through executive order)

MAJOR PROVISIONS
Employers must:
- Furnish workplaces free of recognized hazards
- Comply with health and safety standards

ENFORCEMENT AGENCY
- Occupational Safety and Health Administration (OSHA) (see page 155)

PENALTIES
An employer can be ordered to:
- Pay up to $7,000 per violation (up to $70,000 for a willful or repeat violation)
- Eliminate hazards or pay up to $7,000 per day
- Shut down an operation that is creating an imminent danger

ADDITIONAL INFORMATION
- Employers may not punish employees who complain about safety hazards or file OSHA complaints.
- For life-threatening situations, call 800-321-OSHA.

SAFETY STANDARDS

OSHA health and safety standards are published in the Code of Federal Regulations (CFR).[160] The standards include general and industry-specific rules. OSHA can also issue citations under the general duty clause of the OSH Act, which requires employers to furnish workplaces "free from recognized hazards." Among the standards are requirements that employers:

- Label containers of hazardous chemicals
- Insist that employees wear hard hats, safety shoes, safety glasses, and other personal protective equipment
- Provide protective hearing gear when noise levels exceed 85 decibels for eight hours, and modify equipment when decibel levels exceed 90 decibels
- Maintain workplaces in a clean and orderly condition
- Report accidents that result in fatalities or multiple hospitalizations to OSHA within eight hours
- Log injuries, post annual summaries, and maintain records for five years

OSHA COMPLAINTS

Complaints about safety or health hazards can be filed at OSHA offices or on the OSHA website. Mailing, faxing, or delivering a complaint increases the likelihood of an on-site inspection. Unions can file on behalf of their members.

A box on the complaint form allows an employee to request confidentiality. Nonunion employees should check the box.

Complaints should give a detailed description of the hazard, its location, and the number of persons affected. Describe any requests to the employer to correct the problem.

Illustration. The following is a sample OSHA complaint:

The air-conditioning intakes on the ground floor of Building 29, located at 29 Green Street, are sucking exhaust fumes from test cells into the laser room. The fumes contain carbon monoxide, have a foul odor, and have made two employees ill. The condition has existed for several weeks and affects over twenty employees. The union has notified the company, but it has taken no action to alleviate the hazard.

OSHA either conducts an inspection or sends the complaint to the employer.

TIP: Several techniques improve the chances of an inspection:
- Prior to filing, go over the complaint with an OSHA staffperson.

- Have several employees sign the complaint.
- Send a copy of the complaint to a congressperson or senator.

Inspections. OSHA inspects immediately if a complaint describes a hazard likely to cause death or serious injury. Inspections of lesser hazards may not take place for weeks. The employer is usually not given advance notice. A worker or union representative can accompany the inspector.

Citations. If an investigation confirms a violation, OSHA issues a notice listing the infraction, the amount of the fine, if any, and the time allowed to correct the hazard. The employer must post the citation in a prominent location in the workplace.

National Institute for Occupational Safety and Health

The National Institute for Occupational Safety and Health (NIOSH) (see page 155), an agency of the U.S. Department of Health and Human Services, surveys workplaces where employees have an unusual rate of illness or injury. NIOSH takes a more in-depth look at problems than OSHA.

A group of three employees, or a union, can request a health hazard evaluation on the NIOSH website: www.cdc.gov/niosh. Employee identities are kept confidential. Reports are sent to the requester, the employer, and OSHA. The employer must post the report for thirty days. Employers may not punish employees for making NIOSH requests.

EXAMPLE: Several bank employees experienced dizziness, loss of equilibrium, and headaches. On weekends their symptoms disappeared. When teller Louise Hoffman called OSHA, an inspector referred her to NIOSH. She and two coworkers filed a request for a health hazard evaluation. Four months later, NIOSH discovered that contaminants were entering offices through the steam heat system. The employer agreed to change the system. Employee names were not revealed.

thoughts for change

GOVERNMENT WORKERS

The OSH Act does not apply to state and local government agencies. This means that police, fire, public works, and other government employees are without meaningful safety or health protections. OSHA reimburses states that establish plans covering public employees for up to half of their operating costs. Twenty-six states and territories have taken advantage. Massachusetts should too.

DUTY TO PROVIDE INFORMATION

Employers must inform employees about the chemicals they work with.[161] They must also supply exposure and medical records.

Chemical Hazards

The OSHA Hazard Communications Standard requires employers to:

- Compile a list of hazardous chemicals used in the workplace and make it available to employees and unions.
- Label containers with the names of hazardous chemicals and appropriate warnings.
- Make material safety data sheets (MSDS's) available to employees and unions identifying each hazardous chemical, measures to be taken in the event of exposure, and protective equipment needed for safe handling.
- Implement a hazard communication program and train employees on how to protect themselves from the physical and health hazards of chemicals they work with.
- Inform employees of the standard and its requirements.

NOTE: Labeling is not necessary for portable containers into which chemicals are transferred, provided that the container is intended solely for the immediate use of the employee who performs the transfer.

RIGHT-TO-KNOW LETTER

January 12, 2008

Corney Lindeman
General Manager
Howard Printing Co.
20 Milk St.
Harvard, MA 02612

Dear Mr. Lindeman:

Pursuant to OSHA standard 29 CFR 1910.1200(g)(11), the union requests a list of the technical and common names of each hazardous chemical used in the facility. For each such substance, please attach the MSDS prepared by the manufacturer or distributor.

Yours truly,

Arthur Ruiz, President, Local 100

Exposure Records

Employers must take special measures in workplaces where employees are exposed to toxic substances or harmful physical agents. Toxic substances include chemicals and metals in their liquid, dust, mist, or gaseous forms. Harmful physical agents include excessive noise,

heat, cold, vibration, repetitive motion, radiation, and pressure. Employers must:

- Preserve worker exposure and medical records for thirty years.
- Furnish workers, former workers, and worker representatives with copies of exposure and medical records within fifteen days of request.
- Remind workers annually of the procedure for requesting records.

EXPOSURE RECORDS REQUEST

December 14, 2007

Mr. Richard Appling
New England Thermostats, Inc.
40 Brown St.
Worcester, MA 02243

Dear Mr. Appling:

As provided by OSHA standard 29 CFR 1910.1020, I request the following information:

1. The name of each toxic substance or harmful physical agent to which I have been or am currently exposed in my job as a spray finisher.

2. All records pertaining to my exposure to toxic substances or harmful physical agents, including surveys, monitoring, tests, and other pertinent records.

3. All records pertaining to my medical condition before and after my exposures to toxic substances or harmful physical agents, including medical examinations, tests, and opinions.

4. All background data relevant to understanding and interpreting the results of tests, monitoring, or other studies of my exposures, and any analysis based on such records.

Yours truly,

Felicia Williams

Postings

Employers must display the following information in prominent locations:

- OSHA poster
- Number of occupational injuries and diseases in the prior calendar year (must be posted for the entire month of February)
- Letters from OSHA notifying the company of complaints, and copies of responses
- OSHA citations

WORKER RIGHTS

Employees have a right to demand healthy workplaces without fear of retaliation.

Right to Complain

Employers may not penalize employees who raise concerns about health or safety hazards, report injuries or illnesses, request records, or file complaints with OSHA.

Charges. Retaliation charges must be filed at an OSHA office within thirty days. Unions can file for members. Charges may be filed in person or by fax, telephone, or mail. The safest course is to send the charge by certified mail, return receipt requested. There is no official form.

EXAMPLE: Pam Kaufman told her supervisor on several occasions that fumes at work were making her sick. Instead of fixing the problem, her supervisor said she was a complainer and had her fired. Kaufman filed a retaliation charge with OSHA. After a trial, a federal judge ordered Kaufman reinstated with full back pay.

Right to Refuse

OSHA regulations permit workers to refuse unsafe or unhealthful work assignments under the following circumstances:

1. The worker has a reasonable belief that the assignment poses an imminent threat of death or serious physical injury.

2. The worker asks the employer to eliminate the danger.

3. The danger is so urgent that it would be a risk to wait for OSHA to conduct an inspection.

4. The employee has no reasonable alternative; he or she cannot obtain reassignment to other tasks.[162]

EXAMPLE: Whirlpool Corporation built a mesh screen underneath a high conveyor belt to catch debris. A supervisor told an employee to clean the screen. When he stepped on it, the screen tore and the worker fell twenty feet to his death. A few days later, a supervisor told two other employees to clean the screen. Claiming that the screen was unsafe, the workers refused to carry out the order. Subsequently they received written reprimands. The U.S. Supreme Court ruled that the OSH Act protected the refusals.[163]

TIP: If you refuse work for safety or health reasons, try to have a witness present. Notify your supervisor that you are willing to work at another job or in another location that does not put you in danger. If possible, take a picture of the hazard. If action is taken against you, be sure to file a complaint with OSHA within thirty days.

Truck and bus drivers. The Surface Transportation Assistance Act (STAA) permits drivers of trucks, buses, or other commercial vehicles to refuse to operate vehicles if the operation violates a motor vehicle safety regulation, standard, or order, or if the employee has a reasonable apprehension of serious injury to the employee or the public because of the vehicle's unsafe condition.[164] Before refusing, the operator must report the hazard and give the carrier an opportunity to correct it.

Beyond hazards such as faulty brakes, STAA allows operators to refuse to drive because of marked fatigue, illness, or dangerous road conditions.[165] A driver who is punished for exercising STAA rights must file a discrimination complaint with OSHA within 180 days.[166]

Questions *and* Answers

Listen up

Q: Noise levels in our plant are intolerable. Management provides earplugs but they make it hard to hear. Does the company have to do anything else?

A: Possibly. The OSHA noise standard requires employers to undertake engineering and administrative solutions before requiring earplugs.[167] Engineering solutions include modifying machinery and erecting sound barriers. Administrative solutions include rotating workers away from high-noise areas.

Price of safety

Q: Do employers have to reimburse employees for the purchase of personal protective equipment (PPE) such as steel-toe work shoes?

A: This depends. An OSHA rule issued in November 2007 compels employers to pay for PPE necessary to comply with OSHA standards.[168] PPE includes equipment such as hard hats, hearing protectors, protective gloves, goggles, and face shields.

Ordinary steel-toe shoes or boots are exempted if the shoes can be worn away from the job site. A similar exemption applies to non-specialty prescription eyeglasses. Employers do not have to pay for everyday clothing such as overalls, jackets, rubber boots, winter coats, or cold-weather gloves.

Employee fine

Q: Can OSHA fine workers for unsafe behavior?

A: No.

Violence

Q: I work in a psychiatric hospital. Several workers have been injured by patients. Is there a safety standard that applies to risks of violence?

A: No, but OSHA can use the general duty clause to cite employers that fail to protect employees.

Criminal charges

Q: Three workers suffered lead poisoning after the company ignored warnings from the union. Can we bring criminal charges against the owner?

A: Yes. An employer or manager who recklessly disregards health or safety can be charged with assault and battery or, in the event of death, manslaughter.

Beards and breaths

Q: Management says that since everyone in our department needs to be able to wear respirators, we must shave off our beards and mustaches. Are there any alternatives?

A: Yes. Before making employees wear respirators, employers must consider engineering measures such as installing exhaust equipment.[169]

Chapter Six

Unions

▶ Why Organize?
▶ Union Democracy

Organizing a labor union takes courage and commitment. Nonetheless, the benefits to be gained usually make it worthwhile. Polls suggest that 40 to 50 percent of the U.S. workforce would prefer union representation. Currently only 12.1 percent are organized.

WHY ORGANIZE?

At-will employees (employees without a contract) have a legal status similar to servants. They can be dismissed for arguing with supervisors, criticizing policies, or simply asking too many questions. Wages, duties, and other terms of employment can be altered without explanation or justification. Forming a union is a significant step toward job security.

Another reason to organize is economics. By bringing workers together, unions can pressure employers to increase pay, benefits, and pensions.

A third impetus is to gain a voice. In nonunion workplaces, management decides policies and work rules unilaterally. In organized workplaces, employers must bargain with the union.

Contract Provisions

Unions contracts prevent arbitrary treatment. "Just cause" requirements prohibit employers from disciplining or discharging without justifiable reasons.

Seniority language protects workers with greater service. If a layoff is necessary, less senior employees must be chosen first.

Grievance and arbitration procedures help to resolve disputes. If the parties fail to settle a grievance through discussion, the union can put the matter before a neutral arbitrator whose decision is binding.

The Law of Organizing

The National Labor Relations Act (NLRA), enacted in 1935, guarantees workers in the private sector the right to organize. The act declares that the official policy of the United States is to "encourage the practice and procedure of collective bargaining."[170] The NLRA is enforced by the National Labor Relation Board (NLRB).

NLRB offices are in Boston and Hartford. Unions and employees can file election petitions and unfair-labor-practice charges.

Chapter 150E of the Massachusetts general laws extends similar protections to state and local government employees. Another Massachusetts law, Chapter 150A, covers employers for whom the NLRB declines jurisdiction. Chapters 150E and 150A are enforced by the Massachusetts Division of Labor Relations (DLR).

In Brief
National Labor Relations Act

COVERED EMPLOYERS
* Private sector employers
* U.S. Postal Service

EXCLUDED EMPLOYERS
* Railroads and airlines
* Businesses with yearly revenue less than $500,000
* Race and dog tracks
* Parochial schools

EXCLUDED EMPLOYEES
* Agricultural laborers
* Domestic service employees
* Supervisors
* Persons employed by a parent or spouse

MAJOR PROVISIONS
* Employees may engage in concerted activities to improve their wages and working conditions, including soliciting, petitioning, leafleting, signing union cards, picketing, and striking.
* Unions may petition the National Labor Relations Board (NLRB) to hold an election to certify whether employees want a bargaining representative.
* Employers must bargain in good faith.

ENFORCEMENT AGENCY
* National Labor Relations Board (NLRB) (see page 155)

In Brief
Massachusetts Public Employee Collective Bargaining Law (Chapter 150E)

COVERED EMPLOYERS
- State and local government agencies
- Public educational institutions
- Housing authorities

MAJOR PROVISIONS
- Similar to the NLRA except that employees may not strike or take part in work stoppages.

ENFORCEMENT AGENCY
- Massachusetts Division of Labor Relations (DLR) (see page 154)

Choosing a Union

The first step in organizing is to decide whether to form an independent union or join a national organization. The major advantage of independence is lower dues. The major advantages of a national union are resources such as full-time organizers, educational programs, experienced negotiators, and ties with other unions. Unions can be found in the Yellow Pages under "Labor Organizations" or by contacting the Massachusetts AFL-CIO (see page 159).

> TIP: Don't be misled by titles. Many unions organize occupations and industries that differ from their name. Invite several unions to make presentations to your group.

Campaigns

Union strategies are diverse. Some organizing campaigns are public from the beginning. Others are conducted in secret. A committee is usually formed to manage the campaign.

The law provides two basic paths to representation: persuade the employer to voluntarily recognize the union, or petition a labor agency to hold an election. Both methods require evidence that employees support the union, usually expressed by means of a petition or authorization cards.

AUTHORIZATION CARD

I hereby authorize the _____ Union to be my representative for the purpose of negotiating a collective bargaining agreement with my employer.

Name (print) _____

Name (signature) _____

Date _____

Initials of witness _____

Voluntary recognition. If more than half of the employees sign up, the employer can grant recognition voluntarily. The union may offer to submit its cards to an independent third party. If the employer agrees to this procedure, and the cards are sufficient, the employer must recognize the union and bargain.

NOTE: Under a Massachusetts law enacted in 2007, state and local government agencies must recognize unions which submit authorization cards, petitions, or other evidence showing that a majority of employees in an unrepresented bargaining unit have designated the union as their representative for purposes of collective bargaining.[171] Employers covered by Chapter 150A are also subject to this procedure.

Petition for election. To trigger an election, a union must file authorization cards or a petition signed by at least 30 percent of the employees in the unit being sought.

In the private sector, the union can petition for a trade, a department, a combination of departments, an entire facility, or employees at several facilities. The employees must share a community of interest, that is, enough common working conditions that it makes sense to bargain as a group. In the public sector, large units are favored.

Elections

The weeks preceding an election for union representation are usually hectic. The union campaigns for a Yes vote while the employer urges employees to vote No. Both sides can distribute flyers, hold meetings, and send out mailings.

Unlawful tactics. Some employers, especially in the private sector, go beyond fair debate and engage in illegal threats and bribery. If the union loses because of such tactics, the NLRB may order a new election. In an extreme case, the employer can be ordered to recognize the union. Unlawful tactics include:

- Promising wage increases or special favors if employees vote no
- Threatening to close operations
- Withholding wage increases scheduled before the union campaign began
- Threatening to discharge employees, reduce pay, or eliminate benefits
- Telling employees that the union will need to strike to obtain improvements
- Transferring pro-union employees to undesirable tasks or isolated locations
- Interrogating employees about their union sympathies
- Visiting employees at their homes to ask them to vote against the union.

Retaliation. It is illegal to fire workers for organizing or supporting a union. The union can file unfair labor practice charges seeking reinstatement and back pay.

Election procedures. On election day, NLRB or DLR agents will set up booths for a secret ballot vote. Both parties may have observers, but to avoid intimidation the employer's agent may not be a manager or supervisor. More than 50 percent of the ballots must favor the union. For example, if twenty employees of a twenty-five-member bargaining unit cast ballots, the union needs eleven votes. Once the union's victory is certified, the employer must bargain on a contract.

Bargaining

Success in bargaining depends on member support, negotiation skills, and militance. The vast majority of contracts are settled without a strike. The NLRA requires the parties to:

- Meet frequently as long as there is a possibility of agreement
- Discuss proposals that relate to wages, hours, and conditions of employment
- Provide information needed to understand the issues discussed, including, in some cases, profit and loss data
- Put agreements in writing

Enforcing the Contract

Union contracts usually run for two or three years, though longer periods are common. Most contain a grievance-arbitration procedure to resolve disputes.

Grievance. A grievance is a complaint by the union or an individual worker that the employer has violated the contract or is engaged in other unfair or illegal behavior. Grievance procedures generally involve two or three meetings with management. The union can request documents and data needed to analyze the dispute and present its case.

Arbitration. Many grievances are resolved in the first or second steps. If the employer refuses to settle, the union can refer the case to an outside arbitrator, usually a labor relations specialist. The arbitrator's decision is binding.

UNION DEMOCRACY

A federal law called the Labor-Management Reporting and Disclosure Act (LMRDA or Landrum-Griffen) requires unions to adhere to democratic procedures.[172]

In Brief
Labor-Management Reporting and Disclosure Act

COVERED UNIONS
- Unions whose membership is totally or partially drawn from the private sector
- Unions representing U.S. Postal Service employees

MAJOR PROVISIONS
- Unions may not fine, suspend, expel, or punish members for speaking at union meetings, criticizing union officials, or supporting candidates for union office.
- Unions must follow due process before punishing members for violating rules.
- Union officers must be elected.
- Union officers must obey fiduciary standards.

ENFORCEMENT AGENCY
- Office of Labor-Management Standards, U.S. Department of Labor (see page 155)

PENALTIES
- In the event of election violations, the Department of Labor can order a new vote.
- In the event of disciplinary violations, a court can award injunctive relief, damages, and legal fees.
- In the event of fiduciary violations, a court can impose a sentence of up to to five years and a fine of $10,000.

Free Speech
Title I of the LMRDA guarantees union members the right to criticize union officials, speak up at meetings, and support candidates for

union office. A union may not fine, suspend, expel, refuse to refer for a job, or deny the right to run for office because of a member's expressions. Members may form caucuses, distribute leaflets, wear buttons, and engage in other activities supporting their positions.

The LMRDA does not insulate activities which disrupt union meetings or harm the union as an institution. An example of the latter is a leaflet urging members not to serve on picket duty or to return to work during a strike.

Dues

Dues increases at the local level must be approved by the members through a secret ballot or a mail-in referendum. Unions can increase national dues by means of a convention vote, a membership referendum, or a vote of the national executive board.

Other LMRDA Rights

Union members must be afforded due process in disciplinary proceedings. This includes: notice of charges, a reasonable time to prepare a defense, an unbiased jury, and the right to call witnesses. Fines must be reasonable.

Union Elections

Title IV of the LMRDA regulates union elections.

Local and national officers. Unions must hold elections for constitutional officers such as president, vice president, secretary, and treasurer. Delegates who vote for officers of a national or international union must also be elected. Local unions must conduct elections at least every three years; intermediate bodies at least every four years; and national and international unions at least every five years.

The LMRDA does not require elections for stewards, negotiating committee members, or business agents who do not have executive responsibilities.

Qualifications. Unions may impose reasonable qualifications to run for office, such as regular attendance at meetings. Challengers can contest rules that exclude excessive numbers. The LMRDA bars individuals convicted of certain crimes from holding union office for thirteen years. Disqualifying offenses include assault with grievous bodily injury, embezzlement, extortion, and violations of narcotics laws.

Voting. LMRDA election rules include the following:
- Local unions must elect officers by secret ballot.
- Intermediate bodies must elect officers by secret ballot of members or by delegates chosen by secret ballot.
- National unions must elect officers by secret ballot of members (including a mail-in ballot) or by convention delegates chosen by secret ballot.
- Union funds may not be used to promote candidates.
- Union newspapers may not extol candidates.

Fiduciary Responsibilities

The LMRDA requires that all persons who handle union funds be bonded. Embezzlement, including using union credit cards for private purposes, is punishable by up to five years imprisonment and a $10,000 fine.

Questions *and* Answers

Captive audience

Q: Can a company call a pre-election meeting to force workers to listen to anti-union arguments?

A: Yes, unless the election is scheduled within twenty-four hours.

Next time

Q: If we lose the election, can we submit another petition to the NLRB?

A: Yes, but you must wait twelve months.

Dropping a grievance

Q: I filed a grievance over a promotion. After the company turned it down, the chief steward told me that she is going to withdraw it because "it's a loser." Don't I have a right to have it taken to arbitration?

A: Not necessarily. A union can drop a grievance that lacks merit.

NOTE: A union may not drop a grievance because of a worker's race, gender, sexual orientation, political views, or dues-paying status.

Weingarten rights

Q: My union says I have Weingarten rights. What are they?

A: Weingarten rights allow employees to insist on the presence of a steward or other union representative when interrogated by management.[173] If management denies the request, the worker can refuse to cooperate.

Union security

Q: Is Massachusetts a "right-to-work" state?

A: No. Labor union contracts in Massachusetts can require employees to join unions (union shop) or pay dues (agency shop).

Chapter Seven

Introduction to the Anti-Discrimination Laws

▶ History
▶ Filing Charges
▶ Affirmative Action

Federal and state laws prohibit discrimination in the workplace. Enforced by different agencies, they may seem bewildering. Yet a simple principle unites them: a person has a right to be judged as an individual, not as a member of a stereotyped group.

HISTORY

The Massachusetts Fair Employment Practices Act (FEPA) was enacted in 1946.[174] The original law banned discrimination on the basis of race, color, religion, national origin, and ancestry. Age was added in 1950, sex in 1965, physical and mental handicaps in 1983, sexual orientation in 1989, genetic background in 2000, and military service in 2004. FEPA applies to private sector employers with six or more workers and to public agencies. It is enforced by the Massachusetts Commission Against Discrimination (MCAD).

Congress did not adopt national anti-bias legislation until 1964. Title VII of the Civil Rights Act prohibits discrimination based on race, color, religion, sex, or national origin.[175] Later laws covered physical and mental disabilities and age. Title VII covers private sector employers with fifteen or more employees and public agencies. It is enforced by the Equal Employment Opportunity Commission (EEOC).

In Brief
Massachusetts Fair Employment Practices Act and Title VII

COVERED EMPLOYERS, ORGANIZATIONS, AND AGENCIES
- Private employers with six or more employees
- Public agencies
- Labor organizations
- Employment agencies

EXCLUDED EMPLOYERS
- Tax-exempt membership clubs

MAJOR PROVISIONS
- Employers may not discriminate against job applicants or employees on the basis of race, color, sex, religious creed, national origin, age 40 or over, ancestry, handicap, sexual orientation, genetic background, or military service.
- Hiring or promotion policies that screen out a disproportionate percentage of minorities or women must be justified by a business necessity.

ENFORCEMENT AGENCIES
- Massachusetts Commission Against Discrimination (MCAD) (see page 154)
- Equal Employment Opportunity Commission (EEOC) (see page 153)

PENALTIES
Employers may be ordered to:
- Cease discriminatory practices
- Hire, promote, or restore employment
- Pay back wages and benefits
- Compensate for emotional distress
- Pay punitive damages
- Pay fines of up to $25,000

ADDITIONAL INFORMATION
- Employees must file MCAD or EEOC claims within three hundred days of the last incident of discrimination.
- Employers may not discharge or otherwise punish employees for opposing discriminatory practices, complaining to management, or taking legal action.

FILING CHARGES
Victims of job discrimination often have rights under both FEPA and Title VII. This gives them a choice of filing at the MCAD or the EEOC. Plaintiffs may also sue in court.

thoughts for change

WHY SIX?

The six-employee threshold for coverage by the civil rights laws may have made sense in 1946, but not today. Why should a business that employs five persons be allowed to discriminate on the basis of race or sex? Many other states apply their anti-discrimination laws to small establishments: thirteen cover workplaces with as few as one employee!

Massachusetts Commission Against Discrimination

MCAD procedures are as follows:

1. An MCAD staff member interviews the complainant and helps to fill out a complaint.

2. An investigator holds a conference with the employer and the complainant to clarify the issues and explore settlement.

3. A discovery period may be authorized during which the parties produce documents and answer each other's questions.

4. If the investigation produces evidence that discrimination has occurred, the MCAD issues a finding of probable cause.

5. If settlement attempts are unsuccessful, a hearing is held before a commissioner or hearing officer. The MCAD provides representation for complainants who lack attorneys.

6. The commission issues a decision.

Equal Employment Opportunity Commission

EEOC procedures are as follows:

1. An EEOC staff member interviews the complainant and helps to fill out a complaint.

2. If the agency determines that discrimination has occurred, the EEOC issues a finding of reasonable cause.

3. If settlement attempts are unsuccessful, the EEOC may sue the employer.

TIP: In most cases, the scales tip in favor of the MCAD. Filing with the EEOC is advised if the agency is already suing the employer or if large numbers of employees have been subjected to discrimination (the EEOC can file class-action lawsuits).

ANTICIPATING A DISCHARGE

If you fear being fired for discriminatory reasons:
- Keep a record of comments by supervisors and managers.
- Make a copy of your personnel file.
- Seek commitments from fellow employees to testify if you have to take legal action.

AFFIRMATIVE ACTION

Affirmative action is a concerted effort by an employer to increase the number of women or minorities hired and advanced.

Federal Contractors

Presidential Executive Order 11246 obligates federal government contractors to engage in affirmative action. The Office of Federal Contract Compliance Programs (OFCCP), an agency of the

U.S. Department of Labor, is charged with enforcing the order. The secretary of labor can debar violators.

Written plans. Non-construction contractors that do $50,000 or more in yearly federal business and have fifty or more employees must prepare written affirmative action plans for each of their facilities. The plan must identify departments and positions in which minorities or women are underrepresented and set goals and timetables to eliminate imbalances. The plan must also include provisions covering disabled individuals and veterans.

Construction. Construction contractors and subcontractors must make good faith efforts to reach hiring goals set by OFCCP. The goals apply to all of the contractor's work sites.

The OFCCP goal for women is 6.9 percent of work hours, meaning that contractors must generally attempt to hire one woman for every fourteen men in a craft. Minority goals are based on geographic area and the number of skilled workers available. The goal for Boston, Brockton, Lowell, and Lawrence is 4 percent. In Worcester, Fall River, and New Bedford, the goal is 1.6 percent.

Voluntary Plans

Employers may engage in affirmative action on a voluntary basis in order to address racial or gender imbalances in traditionally segregated job categories. Policies must be narrowly drawn to remedy discrimination and may not require the dismissal or exclusion of whites or males.[174]

Questions *and* Answers

Filing deadline

Q: I grieved my discharge. If I lose at arbitration and more than three hundred days have passed, can I still file an MCAD charge?

A: Yes. The MCAD suspends its filing deadline when an employee pursues a union grievance.[176] You will have three hundred days from the arbitration award to file your complaint.

Religious organization

Q: A religious school told me that I needed to be a member of their order to apply for a teaching position. Isn't this illegal?

A: Not necessarily. Religious organizations can favor applicants from their own religion to perform work connected with the carrying out of the organization's activities.[177]

Solidarity

Q: A friend of mine is circulating a petition alleging that management is mistreating her because of her race. Could I be lose my job for signing?

A: Not legally. Employees may not be fired for opposing practices that they believe are discriminatory.

Genetic test

Q: Our company has instructed keyboard operators to undergo blood tests. They want to screen for a trait that shows a likelihood of developing carpal tunnel syndrome. Legal?

A: No. FEPA forbids employers from demanding genetic tests as a condition of employment or using genetic information to affect a person's job.

Chapter Eight

Race Discrimination

▶ Disparate Treatment
▶ Adverse Impact
▶ National Origin Discrimination

Discrimination against persons of color continues to be widespread despite the civil rights laws. When choosing among applicants of different races, many employers favor white applicants. Discrimination in promotions and assignments is also pervasive, especially with regard to upper level supervisory and managerial positions.

DISPARATE TREATMENT

FEPA and Title VII forbid employers from favoring or disfavoring employees based on race. Discrimination based on skin color is also illegal.

Hiring and Promoting

Unlike nationality, gender, and religion, Title VII does not permit hiring or promoting based on race under any circumstances.[178] If a white person is chosen ahead of a qualified person of color, and the person of color files a discrimination charge, the employer must be able to justify its decision on non-racial grounds.

Evaluations. Employers can base promotions on objective evaluations. To pass as objective, evaluation procedures must take steps to minimize favoritism. Supervisors should be asked to rate employees in defined subject areas rather than offering general opinions.

Assignments

Employers may not consider race in assigning employees. For example, black salespersons cannot be assigned solely to black neighborhoods.

Harassment

Employers must oppose racial or ethnic harassment, including slurs and name-calling. If conditions are intolerable, an employee can resign and sue.

ADVERSE IMPACT

Following Title VII's passage in 1964, some employers turned to indirect methods to screen out minorities. The U.S. Supreme Court considered such techniques in the case of *Griggs v. Duke Power Company*.[179]

For many years Duke, a power-generating corporation in Dan River, North Carolina, flatly refused to transfer black workers from its low-paying labor department. When Title VII became law, the company replaced this policy with a rule requiring transfer applicants to present a high school diploma or pass an aptitude test. Black employees sued, contending that by imposing conditions that few would be likely to meet, the company was effectively keeping them in the labor department.

Duke argued that the transfer rule applied evenly to blacks and whites, but the Supreme Court was not convinced. According to the court, "Neither the high school completion requirement nor the general intelligence test was shown to bear a demonstrable relation-

ship to successful performance of the jobs for which it was used."
Under Title VII, the court declared, policies, practices, or tests that
have an adverse impact on minorities are unlawful unless they are
required by a "business necessity."

Griggs was revolutionary. For the first time minorities were allowed
to file Title VII challenges without having to prove an employer's
intent to discriminate. Since then, *Griggs* has been applied to a host
of selection practices.

Griggs in Practice

Under *Griggs*, a practice that excludes a disproportionate percentage
of minorities from a job or promotion is unlawful unless the employer can prove that the practice is essential to the operation of the
establishment. The employer must also show that no alternative
method would have a less adverse impact while still satisfying the
needs of the business.

High school diploma. Graduation requirements often fail the
Griggs test. Few blue-collar jobs legitimately need a high school
education. Many white-collar jobs, including supervisory positions,
can be safely and efficiently performed without a high school diploma.

Experience. Insisting that applicants have experience in a particular field can have a discriminatory impact on minorities, especially
when entry to the field has historically been limited. When experience is truly needed to ensure safe or efficient performance, it can be
a lawful prerequisite. If experience is only marginally relevant, a
requirement may clash with *Griggs*.

Tests. Aptitude and intelligence tests are lawful if they measure
skills needed for the job in question. For example, restaurant servers
must know basic arithmetic. Tests that go beyond the job and have
a high minority failure rate are often ruled discriminatory.

Seniority. When employers reduce personnel during business
downturns, they sometimes follow seniority procedures, even though
this has an adverse impact on recently-hired minorities and women.
Employees cannot challenge seniority actions under Title VII due to
an exemption in the statute.[180] FEPA has different language than
Title VII and appears to permit a contention that a seniority-based
layoff is discriminatory.[181]

NATIONAL ORIGIN DISCRIMINATION

Employers may not reject applicants because of a person's place of birth or ancestry. For example, an employer cannot reject all applicants from the Middle East or from Latin America. Nor may they deny employment because they perceive a person as looking or sounding "foreign." A narrow exception applies when national origin is an essential qualification, such as a restaurant that needs Chinese chefs for reasons of authenticity.

Citizenship. The Immigration Reform and Control Act (IRCA), applicable to employers with four or more workers, prohibits hiring policies that exclude lawful aliens.[182] Exceptions apply to positions which require citizenship under a law, regulation, or executive order.

No-match letters. IRCA forbids employers from knowingly employing persons who are ineligible to work in the United States. The Social Security Administration (SSA) sends letters to employers and employees when the name or number listed on an employee's W-2 form does not match SSA records.[183] No-match letters do not, in themselves, establish a lack of eligibility, as the letters frequently result from clerical errors or name changes. Employers should investigate further before taking action.

Questions *and* Answers

English only

Q: Can employees be forbidden from speaking languages other than English on the job?

A: Yes, but only if the rule is restricted to conversations for which English is a business necessity, such as when employees are interacting with customers or using dangerous equipment.[184]

Interracial marriage

Q: Three days after I married a black man my boss fired me. Can I file a discrimination complaint even though I am white?

A: Yes. Adverse treatment because an employee enters an interracial marriage violates FEPA and Title VII.

Independent contractor

Q: I am an independent contractor. Supervisors at a company I work for call me names and use racial slurs. Could I quit and sue for racial harassment?

A: Possibly. Although Title VII and FEPA's protections are limited to employees, contractors can sometimes take action under other anti-discrimination laws.[185]

Foreign owner

Q: A Tokyo concern is buying our firm. Rumor has it that they will be replacing the entire front office with Japanese personnel. Would this violate Title VII?

A: Possibly. Replacing employees based on nationality is unlawful unless the employer can show a business necessity for the policy.

Working papers

Q: I was rejected for a job because the interviewer did not believe my working papers were valid. Could I file an IRCA complaint?

A: Yes. Rejecting documents that appear to be genuine may be evidence of illegal discrimination.[186] Call the Office of Special Counsel for Immigration-Related Unfair Employment Practices. (See page 155.)

Chapter Nine

Sex Discrimination

- ▶ Hiring and Promotions
- ▶ Working Conditions
- ▶ Equal Pay
- ▶ Sexual Harassment
- ▶ Sexual Orientation

L abor law in the United States has its ironic side. In the early 1960's Congress was debating a bill to outlaw racial discrimination. Hoping to generate opposition, Southern delegates threw their support behind an amendment to bar sex discrimination as well. To their chagrin, the entire bill passed, becoming the Civil Rights Act of 1964.

HIRING AND PROMOTIONS

Title VII of the Civil Rights Act and Section 4 of the Massachusetts Fair Employment Practices Act (FEPA) forbid employers from discriminating on the basis of sex. Employers cannot favor men in hiring or promotions even if women have never performed the job. Favoritism toward females is similarly prohibited.

Gender may be considered when sex is a "bona fide occupational qualification," but, besides acting roles, the courts generally restrict this exception to correctional officers, delivery room nurses, and other positions carrying heightened privacy concerns. Otherwise, if an employer selects a man over an equally qualified woman, and the woman files a charge at the MCAD or the EEOC, the employer must be able to justify its decision on grounds other than gender.

Stereotyping

Employers may not reject female applicants on the grounds that a job is unsuitable or unsafe. Stereotyping is illegal even if the employer has an honest concern.

Heavy work. Women must be given equal consideration for heavy work jobs. Lifting tests must correspond to duties and be required of all applicants. "Eyeball exams" may not be relied on.

EXAMPLE: Cathy Morris applied for a job as a laborer. Although she had previously performed heavy work, the interviewer rejected her because "you don't look strong enough." Morris can file a discrimination charge.

Danger. Women applicants cannot be rejected because a job is located in a high-crime area or requires entry into customer homes.

Health hazards. Jobs that involve lead or other materials that are hazardous to reproductive health cannot be reserved for males. According to the U.S. Supreme Court, "[D]ecisions about the welfare of future children must be left to the parents who conceive, bear, support and raise them, rather than the employers who hire those parents."[187]

Pregnancy. An employer cannot refuse to hire a woman because she is pregnant. Nor may employment be denied because of the sentiments of coworkers, clients, or customers. The applicant must be able to perform the major functions of the job.

EXAMPLE: On her first day, a marketing manager showed up in a maternity dress. The store withdrew its job offer. The MCAD awarded more than $160,000 in damages.

Discrimination because of pregnancy-related conditions—for example, an abortion—is also unlawful.

Children. Employers may not turn down women with young children based on assumptions that this will lead to attendance problems. Interviewers may not ask female applicants if they plan to have children. Nor may they inquire about child care arrangements.[188]

Illegal Requirements

Height and experience requirements often have a discriminatory impact. Selection practices that disproportionally exclude women must be justified by a business necessity.

Height. In a case against the New Bedford Police Department, a court ruled that a minimum height standard of five feet six inches was unlawful.[189]

Experience. In a case against a railroad, a court ruled that a requirement that apprentice engineers have prior train service was unlawful because it had an exclusionary impact on women.[190]

Appearance. Insisting that female employees have an "attractive appearance" is unlawful unless the employer applies the same standard to males.

WORKING CONDITIONS

Employers must treat males and females equally regarding working conditions such as office space, work rules, assignments, overtime opportunities, training, rest periods, and leaves of absence. The following are violations:

• Giving men better offices than women
• Assigning women to more unpleasant jobs than men
• Supervising women more closely than men
• Ordering women not to talk on the job while allowing men to converse freely
• Telling women to stay at their workstations while allowing men to leave at will
• Denying child care leaves to men when while routinely granting similar requests from women

EQUAL PAY

Two laws target pay discrimination.

Federal Equal Pay Act

The federal Equal Pay Act (EPA), applicable to nearly all employers, prohibits paying female or male employees less than employees of the opposite gender who perform work of an equal character in the same establishment.[191] Exceptions are allowed if the pay disparity is based on job experience, educational background, merit, seniority, skill level, or other non-gender-based factors.

An employer can violate the EPA by paying a woman a lower salary than a man she replaces, paying a man more than a woman he replaces, or paying a predominantly male classification higher wages than a predominantly female classification doing the same type of work. Discrimination does not have to be intentional to constitute a violation.

Enforcement. The EPA is enforced by the Equal Employment Opportunity Commission (EEOC). Investigators do not reveal complainants' names. Employees can sue for up to three years of double back pay.

Massachusetts Equal Pay Act

The Massachusetts Equal Pay Act (MEPA), enforced by the MCAD, is worded slightly differently than the EPA. MEPA insists on wage equality when men and women perform work "of like or comparable character."[192] The only acceptable basis for higher wages is seniority. Though this appears to give the law a wider reach than the EPA, the Massachusetts Supreme Judicial Court has applied MEPA in a narrow fashion.[193]

SEXUAL HARASSMENT

Sexual harassment violates the anti-discrimination laws. It is illegal in two forms.

Quid Pro Quo

Quid pro quo harassment occurs when an employer or a supervisor pressures an employee into sexual activity as a condition of continued employment, advancement, or to retain a job benefit. Examples include promising a promotion if a worker engages in sex or threatening termination to coerce an employee to continue an affair.

Employees who are mistreated because they reject sexual advances can file charges at the EEOC or the MCAD. If conditions are intolerable, the employee can resign and sue.[194] Quid pro quo harassment is unlawful whether directed at females or males, or to members of the same gender as the perpetrator.

Hostile Environment

Hostile environment harassment occurs when supervisors or fellow employees create an intimidating, stigmatizing, or humiliating work environment through touching, bumping, requests for favors, jokes, displays of lewd pictures, questions about sexual experiences, or other unwelcome sexual conduct.

Severity. A single off-color comment, joke, or touch is usually not considered sexual harassment, even if the employee is easily offended. Generally speaking, conduct must be severe and pervasive, and interfere with the employee's job performance.

Paramour favoritism. Some courts have ruled that bestowing favors on subordinates who engage in sexual affairs creates a hostile environment for other workers because it conveys a message that advancement depends on engaging in sex.[195]

Written policy. Employers with six or more employees must distribute policy statements condemning sexual harassment when employees are hired and once a year thereafter. The policy must explain that harassment is forbidden, give examples, outline penalties, provide a procedure for complaints, and direct employees to relevant state and federal agencies.[196]

Employer Liability

An employer's responsibility to pay damages for sexual harassment depends in part on the identity of the perpetrator.

Supervisors. Employers are liable for sexual harassment initiated by supervisors whether or not the victimized employee reports the problem to upper level management.[197] Employers have a duty to ensure that supervisory personnel abide by the law.

Rank-and-file employees. Employers are responsible for harassment by rank-and-file employees if management is aware of or should know of the conduct and fails to take prompt measures.

Nonemployees. Similarly, employers are held responsible for harassment by clients, customers, and contractors if management knows of or should know of the conduct and fails to take prompt measures.

EXAMPLE: Two regular customers made life miserable for Carol Fortson, a hotel waitress. When Fortson complained to her boss about their lewd comments, he laughed it off. Fortson can sue the hotel because of her supervisor's inaction.

Small companies. Employees of establishments with fewer than six employees can sue for sexual harassment under Chapter 214 of the Massachusetts Code.[198]

CHALLENGING HARASSMENT

Faced with sexual harassment, an employee should:
- Tell the perpetrator to stop
- Keep a log of dates, times, descriptions, and witnesses
- Inform upper-level managers and insist that action be taken

---

SEXUAL ORIENTATION

The Massachusetts Fair Employment Practices Act (FEPA) prohibits discrimination based on sexual orientation. It is illegal to:
- Fire or refuse to hire an individual because the person self-identifies as gay or because the employer so identifies the individual
- Treat a gay employee more harshly than a heterosexual employee in regard to lateness, absenteeism, or other work infractions
- Abuse or harass an employee because the employee is gay, is considered gay, or has a history of homosexuality
- Discharge an employee because customers claim to be offended by the employee's sexual orientation

Questions *and* Answers

Recent experience requirement

Q: I was turned down for a job for lack of experience. I worked in the field after college but stopped ten years ago to bring up my children. Company policy requires work in the field within the prior five years. Could I file an MCAD charge?

A: Yes. You could argue that requiring recent experience is discriminatory because women are more likely than men to temporarily leave the workforce.[199]

Ending affair

Q: If I break off a relationship with my boss and he fires me, would I have a good claim for sexual harassment?

A: Not necessarily. A manager who fires an employee because of hurt feelings or embarrassment, but not to force the employee to continue sexual activity, does not commit actionable harassment.

Reverse discrimination

Q: A man and a woman fought on the job. The company fired the man but not the woman. Can the man sue?

A: Yes. The anti-discrimination laws prohibit favoritism for either gender.

Work during pregnancy

Q: Can my boss force me to go on leave when my pregnancy enters the ninth month?

A: No, unless valid medical evidence establishes that you can no longer perform your duties.

Profanity

Q: My boss frequently uses language that I consider disgusting, including the "f" word. Could I sue for sexual harassment?

A: Probably not. Profanity, even when extreme, is usually not considered sexual harassment unless it is directed exclusively at women or is charged with sexual innuendo.

Dress code

Q: Our company requires men to wear ties and jackets but allows women to dress as they please. Legal?

A: Yes. Dress code differences generally do not violate the gender discrimination laws.[200]

No-spouse rule

Q: Company policy rejects job applicants who are married to current employees. Legal?

A: Possibly. No-spouse policies are lawful if applied evenhandedly to men and women and not to perpetuate an all-male or all-female workforce.

Sex change

Q: Can a company fire a worker because he changes his gender from male to female?

A: No. As construed by the MCAD, FEPA prohibits discrimination against transsexuals.[201]

Busted

Q: In a Seinfeld episode a few years ago a restaurant rejected Elaine because of her bust size. Could Elaine have sued?

A: Yes. Although the anti-discrimination laws do not list appearance as a disfavored classification, Elaine could have argued that male applicants would not have been judged by their sexual appeal.

Chapter Ten

Age Discrimination

▶ Hiring
▶ Terms of Employment

The federal Age Discrimination in Employment Act (ADEA)[202] and the Massachusetts Fair Employment Practices Act (FEPA) prohibit discrimination against workers age 40 and older. FEPA apples to employers with six or more workers.[203] Complaints must be filed at the EEOC or the MCAD within three hundred days.

HIRING

In the absence of a bona fide occupational qualification, rejecting an applicant who is 40 or older because of his or her age is illegal. It is likewise unlawful to favor a younger applicant because of youth. Employers must give older applicants the same consideration as younger ones, even if job duties are strenuous.

EXAMPLE: Howard Williams, age 60, applied for a maintenance position. The interviewer turned him down, saying, "A man your age could never handle the job." Williams can sue for age discrimination.

Advertisements

Help-wanted advertisements may not express preferences for young workers. The following solicitations cross the line: "Sales position, early twenties preferred"; "Looking for bright young man or woman"; "Counter boy wanted"; "Maximum 2 to 5 years experience"; "Prefer college student"; "Recent grad desired."

Pre-employment Inquiries and Examinations

Neither the ADEA nor FEPA categorically forbid employers from asking for an applicant's age or date of birth. However, MCAD regulations describe such questions as impermissible unless age is a bona fide occupational qualification.[204] An employer required to conduct a CORI check can solicit date of birth information in order to fill out the request form. Employers may not ask older applicants to submit to physicals unless they also require examinations of younger applicants.[205]

TERMS OF EMPLOYMENT

Employers may not discriminate against older workers with regard to conditions or terms of employment.

Promotions

Promotions may not be withheld because of age or a worker's proximity to retirement.

EXAMPLE: Harvey Prince, a 64-year-old history teacher, applied for a high-level administrative position. The superintendent turned him down because he had one year to go before retirement age. Prince can sue for age discrimination.

Harassment

Supervisors may not abuse workers because of their age. Repetitious joking, unfavorable assignments, excessive scrutiny, or disproportionate discipline creates a hostile work environment.

Layoffs

A company that reduces its workforce for economic reasons may not select older employees on the theory that their age makes them less valuable. Nor may an employer select employees for layoffs because they are eligible for retirement.

Mandatory Retirement

It is generally illegal to force employees to retire because of their age. The following are exceptions:

- Executives and other high-level policymaking employees may be forced to retire at age 65 or higher if their retirement benefits will be at least $44,000 per year and they have been in their positions for two years or longer.
- Police, firefighters, and other public safety personnel can be forced to retire at ages specified in state or local laws.[206]
- Government employees can be forced to retire at ages set in retirement laws.
- An employer can force employees to retire at a particular age if it can prove that at this age most individuals cannot meet the physical or mental demands of the job and that reviewing employees individually would be impractical.[207]

Incentives. Employers can offer lump-sum payments or increased pensions to encourage employees to retire—if the incentives are offered to employees both above and below retirement age. Employers may not coerce employees to accept "golden handshakes."

Questions *and* Answers

Selections by salary level

Q: Corporate has issued a directive that each department lay off their three highest-paid employees. In almost every case this will affect persons older than 50. Isn't this age discrimination?

A: Not necessarily. The U.S. Supreme Court has ruled that a policy that has a disproportionate impact on older workers is lawful if it has a "reasonable basis."[208]

Overtime

Q: Our supervisor gives all the overtime assignments to the younger workers. Legal?

A: No. Older workers are entitled to the same job opportunities as younger workers.

Health benefits

Q: Can an employer reduce health coverage for retirees when they become eligible for Medicare?

A: Possibly. A 2007 federal regulation exempts Medicare offset policies from the ADEA.[209] It remains to be seen whether Massachusetts will follow suit in enforcing FEPA.

Chapter Eleven
Disability Discrimination

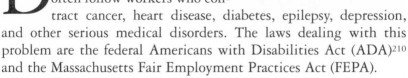

▶ Defining Disability
▶ Discharges
▶ Duty to Accommodate

Discharges and job rejections often follow workers who contract cancer, heart disease, diabetes, epilepsy, depression, and other serious medical disorders. The laws dealing with this problem are the federal Americans with Disabilities Act (ADA)[210] and the Massachusetts Fair Employment Practices Act (FEPA).

These laws prohibit discrimination in hiring, promotions, and discharges against a person with a disability if the person can perform the essential functions of the job he or she is seeking. Employers must make reasonable changes in duties, equipment, hours, location, and other aspects of jobs to enable disabled employees to work.

In Brief
State and Federal Disability Laws

COVERED EMPLOYERS AND ORGANIZATIONS
- Private sector employers with six or more employees
- Public agencies
- Labor organizations

EXCLUDED EMPLOYERS
- Tax-exempt membership clubs

MAJOR PROVISIONS
- Employers may not discriminate against qualified individuals with disabilities.
- Employers must make reasonable accommodations.

ENFORCEMENT AGENCIES
- Massachusetts Commission Against Discrimination (MCAD) (see page 154)
- Equal Employment Opportunity Commission (EEOC) (see page 153)

PENALTIES
Employers may be ordered to:
- Stop discriminatory practices
- Hire, promote, or restore employment
- Make reasonable accommodations
- Pay back wages and related benefits
- Pay damages for emotional pain
- Pay punitive damages

ADDITIONAL INFORMATION
- Complaints must be filed with the MCAD or the EEOC within three hundred days of a violation.
- Employers may not discharge or punish employees who request accommodations, file complaints, or sue in court.

DEFINING DISABILITY

Although the ADA protects persons with "disabilities" and the FEPA protects persons with "handicaps," both terms have the same meaning. For simplicity, this chapter uses the term disability.

An individual is considered to have a disability if he or she 1) has a long-term or potentially long-term physical or mental impairment that substantially limits one or more major life activities; or 2) has a record of such impairment even if no impairment currently exists; or 3) is regarded as having such impairment even if no impairment exists.

Major Life Activities

Major life activities include walking, standing, speaking, seeing, hearing, breathing, sleeping, lifting, reaching, concentrating, caring for oneself, interacting with others, engaging in sexual relations, performing manual tasks, and working.

An employee is substantially limited in working if an impairment prevents him or her from performing a broad range of jobs in various classes or precludes an entire class of jobs, such as clerical, manual, or heavy work.

EXAMPLE: Carol Lewis suffers stress-induced angina. Because the condition prevents her from performing a broad range of jobs in various classes, she qualifies as an individual with a disability.

EXAMPLE: A hand disorder prevents Arthur Rankin from using a keyboard. Since this precludes an entire class of work, he qualifies as a person with a disability.

NOTE: FEPA assesses the extent to which an impairment limits a major life activity without regard to mitigating measures such as medications or therapeutic devices.[211] An individual who takes medications is disabled if, left untreated, his or her impairment would meet the disability tests.

Occupational Injuries

Persons who sustain occupational injuries have special rights. Section 75B of the Massachusetts Workers' Compensation Act provides that:

Any employee who has sustained a work-related injury and is capable of performing the essential functions of a particular job, or who would be capable of performing the essential functions of such job with reasonable accommodations, shall be deemed to be a qualified handicapped person.

Section 75B extends FEPA status to many conditions that might not ordinarily qualify as disabilities.[212] For example, an employee who sprains an ankle on the job may have a right to a new schedule or other accommodations even though the condition is expected to resolve within weeks.

DISCHARGES

Employers cannot discharge persons who develop disabilities if they can perform their essential job functions, with accommodations if necessary.

Employment can be denied if the employee poses a "direct threat" to himself or others. A direct threat is a significant risk of substantial harm that cannot be eliminated or reduced through a reasonable accommodation.

Harassment. Supervisors may not harass persons who develop disabilities or who are provided accommodations. In extreme cases an employee can resign and sue.

Disparate impact. Company policies—such as qualification standards, tests, or other selection criteria—that have a disparate impact on persons with disabilities must serve a business necessity.

DUTY TO ACCOMMODATE

Both FEPA and the ADA require employers to make reasonable accommodations to disabled applicants and current employees. Accommodations include special equipment, adjusted duties, modified schedules, assistance by co-employees, and other changes that will enable the individual to perform the essential functions of a job. Unless a need is obvious, the individual must make a request to the employer or the employer's agent.[213] Employers can ask for documentation of a disability and its functional limitations. The duty to accommodate applies to all employees including new and part-time workers.

In determining whether there is a duty to accommodate, employers must address the following questions:

1. Does the individual have a disability?
2. Will an accommodation enable the individual to perform the essential duties of the position sought or held?
3. Will the accommodation impose an undue hardship?

Does the Individual Have a Disability?

As discussed above, the duty to accommodate applies to persons whose impairments substantially limit a major life activity, persons with a history of such an impairment, persons who are perceived as having such limitations, and persons who have incurred occupational injuries.

Will an Accommodation Enable the Individual to Perform His or Her Essential Duties?

Accommodations are only required if they will enable a disabled individual to execute the essential or fundamental duties of a position.[214] A truck driver must be able to drive; a professor must be able to teach. Employers have no obligation to hire or retain employees who, even with accommodations, are unable to perform the basic duties of a position.

Illustrations. Examples of reasonable accommodations include:

- Allowing an employee with multiple chemical sensitivities to work at home
- Permitting periodic breaks for an employee with ADHD
- Allowing an employee with cancer to take leave for six months
- Providing air conditioning for an employee with a respiratory condition
- Permitting an employee with a psychiatric disorder to work part-time
- Allowing an employee with leg braces to use an executive parking space
- Providing a reader for a blind employee

NOTE: An employer does not always have to make the change requested by the employee; it may, for example, choose a less expensive option that produces the same result.

Transfer. Sometimes there is no accommodation that will enable an employee to perform his or her current position. For example, a nurse with arthritis may not be able to lift patients even with assistance. In such cases the employer can assign the employee to a new position.[215]

A worker who cannot remain in his or her original position can insist on a transfer to another position if the position is vacant and the worker is qualified, with accommodations if necessary, to perform its duties.[216] Creating a new position is not required. Nor must an employer lower production standards to facilitate a transfer.

Will the Accommodation Cause an Undue Hardship?

Employers do not have to make accommodations that would create an undue hardship for the establishment. An undue hardship is a significant difficulty or expense considering the employer's resources and the nature of its operations. An accommodation that is reasonable for a large company may be unreasonable for a small one.

Tax credits. Employers who incur expenses to accommodate disabled workers can qualify for yearly tax credits of up to $5,000 and deductions of up to $15,000. Tax savings must be considered before an employer claims that a change will create a financial hardship.

Conflict with seniority system. Employers do not have to make accommodations that violate the rules of an established and enforced seniority system, whether union negotiated or unilaterally established.[217] For example, an employer can refuse to transfer an individual to a vacant position if a more senior employee has a right to the opening.

Burden on others. The ADA does not require an accommodation that forces other employees to work harder or longer or that disrupts their work.[218]

Interactive process. An employer that rejects an accommodation as an undue hardship must initiate an interactive dialogue with the employee regarding other possible accommodations.[219]

Questions *and* Answers

Lifting

Q: Due to my arthritic condition, my doctor has placed me on a permanent twenty-pound lifting restriction. The only way I can keep my job is if the company buys me a forklift. Do I qualify as disabled?

A: Yes. Guidelines issued by the MCAD list lifting as a major life activity.[220]

Double play

Q: Six months ago I suffered a heart attack. Management is refusing to make changes in my job. If I file for Social Security Disability Insurance (SSDI), can I still sue for reinstatement?

A: Yes. Persons claiming disability under social security or workers' compensation can pursue claims contending that, with accommodations, they could perform the essential duties of a job.[221]

Perceived disability

Q: An employee missed work for ten weeks after wrenching her knee in an auto accident. Even though her condition fully resolved and her doctor cleared her to work, her manager refused to reinstate her because he was concerned that she would have another injury. Violation?

A: Possibly. Workers regarded as handicapped by their employers qualify for protection under the disability laws—even if their conditions are no longer disabling.

Reactions of others

Q: I need a longer break because of my heart condition. But the general manager said that if he does this for me, everyone will want one. Is this a legitimate reason to deny my request?

A: No. Concerns about the reactions of others are not a lawful basis to deny accommodations to a disabled employee.

Extended leave

Q: I need eight months off to have surgery for cancer. Company policy limits leaves to six months. Do I have any rights under the ADA?

A: Yes. A leave of absence that enables an employee to receive medical treatment is a reasonable accomodation if an employee has a good prospect of recovery.[222]

HIV

Q: Can I be fired if management finds out that I am HIV-positive?

A: No. HIV infection is a disability, even if you are asymptomatic.[223] You must be allowed to work as long as you can perform your essential duties.

Alcoholism

Q: Can an alcoholic worker be fired for causing an accident while under the influence?

A: Yes. Though alcoholism is a medical disorder, a provision in the ADA allows employers to hold alcoholics to the same standards as other employees, even if the employee's misbehavior is related to the disorder.[224]

Chapter Twelve

Unemployment Insurance

▶ Benefits
▶ Exclusions
▶ Discharges, Resignations, Strikes
▶ Hearings

Congress created the unemployment insurance (UI) system in 1935. States establish eligibility requirements and benefit levels within federal parameters. Employers fund the programs through quarterly payments. The Massachusetts system is administered by the Division of Unemployment Assistance (DUA).

Businesses are charged for each employee who uses the system. Called "experience rating," this creates an incentive for employers to attempt to disqualify workers or to argue that they are independent contractors.

In Brief

Massachusetts Unemployment Insurance System

COVERED EMPLOYEES
- Private sector workers
- Government workers

MAJOR PROVISIONS
- Employees who lose their jobs through no fault of their own are eligible for weekly benefits.
- Employees who are fired for deliberate misconduct or who quit voluntarily are disqualified.

ENFORCEMENT AGENCY
- Massachusetts Division of Unemployment Assistance (DUA) (see page 154)

ADDITIONAL INFORMATION
- Employers must give separated employees, including employees who are discharged or resign, a DUA pamphlet entitled "How to File for Unemployment Insurance Benefits."
- Employees may initiate claims at DUA walk-in centers or by calling 877-626-6800.

BENEFITS

Eligible claimants can qualify for up to thirty weeks of benefits. A one-week waiting period must be served.

Eligibility Requirements

To qualify for UI benefits a claimant must:

1. Be unemployed through no fault of his or her own;

2. Have earned at least $3,000 and worked at least fifteen weeks over the prior year; and

3. Be capable of, available for, and actively seeking work.

Weekly Rate

The benefit rate is approximately half of average weekly wages, up to a maximum.[225] For the twelve-month period beginning October 1, 2007, the maximum rate was $600. Payments are rounded down to the closest dollar.

> **EXAMPLE:** Max Runyan's average weekly wage is $601.80. His benefit rate is $300.

Dependents. An allowance of $25 is added for each dependent child.[226]

> **EXAMPLE:** Nadine Moore's benefit rate is $525. She has three children under age 18. Her dependency allowance is $75 per week.

Part-time work. If a claimant takes part-time work, DUA subtracts the difference between gross earnings and one-third of the benefit rate. Put another way: a claimant can earn up to one-third of his benefit rate without having his benefits reduced.

> **EXAMPLE:** Sam Costello's benefit rate is $450. If he takes a part-time job paying $150 per week, his UI check will not be reduced. If he takes a job paying $200, DUA will reduce his check by $50.

Duration. Normally, the maximum number of weeks a claimant can collect full benefits is thirty. Claimants laid off due to a plant closing can collect an additional thirteen weeks. Claimants who participate in a vocational or educational training program can collect an additional eighteen weeks.

Taxes. UI benefits are taxable. If requested, DUA withholds 10 percent for federal taxes and 5.3 percent for state taxes.

Employer contribution rates. Employers fund UI benefits by paying a quarterly tax or "contribution" on the first $14,000 in wages of each employee.[227] The contribution rate is based in part on UI benefits paid to employees over the prior year.

> **TIP:** Persons who inform DUA about employers who fail to pay their proper contributions—for example, by deliberately misclassifying employees as independent contractors or underreporting payroll—may be awarded a 10 percent "whistleblower reward."[228] The fraud hotline number is 1-800-354-9927.

Health Benefits

Under federal and state COBRA laws (see page 42), workers who lose their jobs can stay in group health plans by paying the full premium plus 2 percent. Two DUA programs can help. Premium Assistance provides UI claimants with up to $790 a month for a family plan and $360 a month for an individual plan (2007 rates). Direct Coverage covers claimants who are not part of a health plan. Income limits apply.

Severance and Vacation Pay

Severance and vacation pay can affect benefits.

Severance pay. Severance payments are usually treated as wages. If the payment is made in a lump sum, UI benefits are deferred for a matching number of weeks.

> **EXAMPLE:** Jill Brooks was laid off after twelve years of service. Under company policy she received a severance check equal to twelve weeks of pay. Brown can open a DUA claim, but her checks will not begin for thirteen weeks: twelve weeks plus the waiting period. She can then collect for up to thirty weeks.

Severance pay is not treated as wages if it is paid pursuant to a plant closing, a corporate takeover, or on condition that the employee signs a release of claims.[229]

Vacation pay and medical insurance. Vacation pay generally does not affect UI benefits. However, if a claimant has a firm recall date, DUA may treat the allowance as wages. Medical insurance contributions do not affect UI benefits.

Search for Work

UI claimants are expected to make a minimum of three work-search contacts each week and to keep a log of their efforts. Claimants who fail to conduct active searches may be suspended. Claimants who incur illnesses or injuries can defer searches for up to three weeks while they recover.

Availability. Claimants may express preferences for particular hours or shifts, but must accept work at other times unless constrained by good cause, such as compelling family responsibilities. In limited circumstances a claimant can restrict a search to part-time work, such as when the employee has a disability or a history of working part time for good reason. Refusing work without good cause is grounds for disqualification for up to eight weeks.

Suitable work. Suitable work includes work in the claimant's regular occupation and other work that the claimant is equipped to perform. The work must be within a reasonable commuting distance, must not be available due to a strike or other labor dispute, and must have a compensation rate at or above the claimant's previous level.[230]

False statements. Falsifying work searches, earnings, or other UI matters can lead to criminal prosecution. Claimants who collect benefits fraudulently can be ordered to repay two weeks of benefits for each week of overpayment.

EXCLUSIONS

The UI law excludes several occupations. The largest category is independent contractors.

Independent Contractors

Persons in business for themselves are not eligible for UI benefits. Employers sometimes use this rule to try to challenge claimants. The UI law makes it difficult to establish the exclusion. To qualify a claimant as an independent contractor, an employer must establish the following facts:

1. The claimant performed his or her work free from control and direction by the employer.

2. The claimant provided services outside of the usual course of the employer's business or away from its premises.

3. The claimant was engaged in an independently established trade, profession, or business.

Other Exclusions

Other exclusions in the UI law include: medical interns; elected officials; legislators; judges; policymakers; newspaper deliverers younger than 18; work-study jobholders at colleges and universities; real estate brokers; insurance agents working on commission; cooperative education students; prison inmates; employees of religious organizations; noncitizens without work authorizations; railway workers; children younger than 18 employed by parents; parents employed by children; spouses employed by spouses (unless the business is incorporated); camp counselors; sole proprietors; and members of partnerships.

School Employees

Teachers, professors, custodians, and other employees of educational institutions are disqualified from UI benefits during the summer, between semesters, and during vacation breaks. Schools must provide reasonable assurances that the employee will be employed in the same capacity after the break.

DISCHARGES, RESIGNATIONS, STRIKES

Employees who are discharged, who resign, or who are out of work due to a strike may be disqualified from UI benefits.

Discharges

The UI law disqualifies employees who are fired for deliberate misconduct or for knowingly violating a reasonable and uniformly enforced rule.

Disqualifying offenses. Discharges for the following reasons are generally disqualifying:

- theft
- dishonesty
- absence without good cause after a warning
- absence without giving notice as required by company rules
- falsification of records
- chronic tardiness after a warning
- falsification of important parts of a job application
- refusal of assigned work without good cause
- insubordination (other than minor arguments)
- harassment
- deliberate lack of effort
- neglect that causes substantial damage to the employer's property
- sleeping on the job

- fighting
- conviction of a crime
- possession or use of drugs
- failure to return after a leave of absence

State of mind. State of mind is important in discharge cases. The employer must establish that misconduct was intentional. Involuntary or accidental violations are not disqualifying. Factors such as provocation, stress, fatigue, or irregular enforcement of company rules may suggest that the employee's actions were not deliberate.

Other offenses. Discharges for the following reasons are generally not disqualifying:

- incompetence
- bad judgement
- inattention
- inability to do the work
- personality conflicts
- unsatisfactory performance
- policy differences
- minor arguments
- bad attitude
- conduct resulting from domestic violence

Resignations

Employees who voluntarily resign from work are not eligible for UI benefits. It is significant, however, that quitting work for justifiable work reasons or because of compelling personal needs is not considered voluntary.

Justifiable work reasons. Employees who resign for the following reasons may be awarded benefits:

- Intolerable or hazardous working conditions
- Permanent or indefinite transfer to work outside the employee's job classification that does not use the employee's highest skills
- Permanent or indefinite transfer to positions for which full-time work is not available
- Severe sexual, racial, or other harassment
- Movement of operations to an area beyond commuting distance
- Excessive demands for overtime
- Late wage payments

- Substantial reductions in wages or benefits
- Reassignment to work that is significantly different from and less attractive than originally promised
- Permanent or indefinite transfer to a shift for which no suitable transportation is available

> TIP: Claimants should attempt to resolve job problems before resigning. If you fail to give your employer an opportunity, DUA may view your resignation as voluntary. Put your complaints in writing whenever possible.

Compelling personal reasons. The UI law does not disqualify claimants who resign for "urgent, compelling, and necessitous" personal reasons. Compelling personal reasons usually relate to overwhelming medical or domestic problems for which the employer refuses to approve a leave of absence. Employees who resign for the following reasons can qualify for benefits:

- Relatives who help with day care are no longer available.
- A relative requires long-term care during working hours.
- A spouse or person with whom the employee has a relationship threatens domestic violence on the employee's route to work.
- A medical problem prevents the employee from performing his or her regular job duties, no other suitable work is available, and either the condition is permanent or the employer refuses to approve a leave of absence.

> NOTE: Before resigning a worker should request a leave of absence unless he or she knows it will not be granted or will not solve the problem.

> FURTHER NOTE: Despite personal problems, UI claimants must be capable of, available for, and actively seeking work which matches their training and experience.

Disqualifying resignations. Claimants who resign because of reprimands from supervisors, to go to school, because of personality conflicts, because an employer refuses to give a wage increase, to start their own business, to search for new employment, or because they dislike their work are usually disqualified. A failure to return to work after a medical or other leave, without explaining the reasons, is usually treated as a voluntary separation.

Strikes and Lockouts

Employees who take part in a union strike are disqualified in most but not all circumstances. The pivotal factor is the impact on operations.

Stoppage. Strikers are not eligible for UI benefits if their walkout is causing a "stoppage of work."[231] They are eligible if operations are maintained.

EXAMPLE: When telephone workers went on strike, supervisors took over their duties. Because there was only a small drop in calls handled, DUA awarded benefits.

To constitute a stoppage, operations must be substantially curtailed. Though the UI law does not state a percentage, it appears that at least a 25 percent reduction is necessary.[232]

EXAMPLE: In the first month of a strike at Zemco Plastics, production was 10 percent as compared to the previous year. In the second month, production rose to 50 percent. In the third month, production rose to 80 percent. At this point, the strikers qualified for UI benefits.[233]

Lockout. Employees who are locked out of work by their employer are eligible for UI benefits unless the lockout is in response to sabotage or threats of sabotage by members of the bargaining unit. The employees must be willing to work under the terms and conditions of their existing or expired contract pending the negotiation of a new agreement.[234]

HEARINGS

A worker whose UI claim is denied can request a hearing before a DUA review examiner. The request must be submitted within ten days. The examiner may rule that the employer presented insufficient evidence or that the local DUA office incorrectly applied the UI law.[235]

Representation

Attorneys or union officers can represent claimants at DUA hearings.

Low-income workers may be able to obtain free representation through a community legal services program. For referrals, call the Legal Advocacy and Resource Center (see page 159).

Questions *and* Answers

Mutual agreement

Q: My boss is letting me go because she doesn't like the way I handle my assignments. She says I can resign to protect my record. If I do, will I be able to collect unemployment insurance?

A: Yes. A resignation to avoid an imminent discharge is not disqualifying unless the termination would have been for misconduct. To clarify that you are not quitting voluntarily, write a note that you are resigning by mutual agreement and ask your boss to sign it.

On-call worker

Q: I am a substitute teacher. Some weeks I work five days, others one or two, and some not at all. Should I be signing up for UI benefits?

A: Yes, but only for weeks you are not called. Unlike workers with full schedules, on-call workers cannot collect UI benefits for short weeks.

Temp agency

Q: Can employees of temporary help firms collect UI benefits between assignments?

A: Yes, but if the agency instructs employees to contact headquarters for new assignments when jobs end, employees must comply before opening UI claims.[236]

Unemployed and pregnant

Q: I have been collecting benefits for three months. Will DUA disqualify me if it finds out I'm expecting?

A: Not if you continue searching for work.

Workers' compensation

Q: After eighteen months on workers' compensation, I settled my case. My company is out of business. Can I collect UI benefits?

A: Yes. UI claimants must usually have worked at least fifteen of the fifty-two weeks before filing, but in the case of workers' compensation DUA credits earnings over the previous two years.

Notice of resignation

Q: I told my boss I was quitting in two weeks to go to school. She responded by firing me immediately. Can I collect UI benefits?

A: Yes, but only for the two weeks you lost from work.

Chapter Thirteen

Workers' Compensation

▶ Covered Conditions
▶ Benefits
▶ Procedures
▶ Returning to Work

The Massachusetts workers' compensation program, created in 1911, assists employees who are injured on the job or who suffer occupational illnesses. The program, which provides income replacement, medical coverage, and retraining, is administered by the Massachusetts Department of Industrial Accidents (DIA). Offices are in Boston, Fall River, Lawrence, Springfield, and Worcester.

In Brief
Massachusetts Workers' Compensation Act

COVERED EMPLOYEES
- Private sector workers
- Government workers

EXCLUDED
- Police officers and firefighters[237]
- Longshore, harbor, and shipyard workers[238]
- Maritime and railroad workers[239]
- Household workers employed for fewer than sixteen hours a week
- Independent contractors

MAJOR PROVISIONS
- Employers must purchase workers' compensation insurance or qualify as self-insurers.
- Insurers must pay benefits to injured workers.
- Employers and supervisors are given immunity from negligence lawsuits.

ENFORCEMENT AGENCY
- Massachusetts Department of Industrial Accidents (DIA) (see page 154)

ADDITIONAL INFORMATION
- Employers must post notices listing the names and addresses of insurance carriers.
- Employers may not punish employees who file claims or testify in DIA proceedings.

COVERED CONDITIONS

The compensation system covers injuries and illnesses that arise out of and in the course of employment. Employees are entitled to benefits even if they are at fault.

Incidents of Employment

Coverage applies from the moment an employee enters the employer's property to the moment he or she departs, whether or not the employee is engaged in work. Examples of compensable injuries include accidents in company parking lots and falls during rest breaks.

Commuting

Generally speaking, the compensation act does not cover injuries and accidents while traveling to and from work. Exceptions apply if a worker is:

- Making a special trip to the workplace before or after regular hours to help the employer meet its responsibilities
- Fatigued because of an excessive amount of required overtime
- Traveling from one worksite to another

Chronic Trauma

Injuries from repetitive work activities are compensable. Examples: carpel tunnel syndrome from keyboard use and a hernia from continuous straining.

Aggravations of Underlying Conditions

If a job incident combines with a preexisting medical condition which is not work-related, a disability that results is compensable if the job incident is a "major cause."[240] If the preexisting condition is work-related, a disability is covered even if the work incident simply hastens its onset. Examples: an employee with a bad back ruptures a disc while reaching for a tool; an employee with a lung disorder develops emphysema from dusty work.

Occupational Diseases

Diseases triggered by work are compensable. Examples: cancer caused by exposure to vinyl chloride; bronchitis caused by benzene fumes.

Contagious Diseases

Contagious diseases are compensable if a hazard of contracting the disease is inherent in the employee's work. Examples: tuberculosis contracted by a nurse in a TB ward; hepatitis contracted by a laboratory worker.

Heart Attack

Coronary infarctions caused by physical or emotional stresses on the job are compensable. Examples include heart attacks precipitated by heavy lifting, rushing up stairs, or arguing with supervisors.

Emotional Disorders

Depression, hysteria, nervous breakdowns, and other emotional disorders are compensable if the predominant cause is an event or series of events on the job. Examples: anxiety attack after a confrontation with a supervisor; depression brought on by harassment.

NOTE: Emotional disorders triggered by personnel actions— investigations, transfers, layoffs, reassignments, discharges— are not compensable unless the employer acted for illegitimate reasons.

BENEFITS

The compensation system pays several categories of benefits.

Temporary Total Incapacity

Most workers are initially paid temporary total incapacity (TTI) benefits.

Waiting period. An employee is eligible for TTI benefits if an injury disables him or her for six or more calendar days, including weekends and days off. Payments begin as of day six. If the disability lasts twenty-one days, the employee is paid for the initial five days.

EXAMPLE: Bob Stone was injured on Wednesday and returned to work on the following Monday. He is not entitled to TTI benefits because he was only disabled for five calendar days.

EXAMPLE: Paul Winger was disabled for ten days. He is entitled to benefits for days six through ten.

EXAMPLE: Erica Davis was disabled for twenty-eight days. The insurer must pay for the entire period.

Rate. The TTI benefit is 60 percent of average gross weekly wages up to a maximum rate. The maximum rate is the statewide average weekly wage in effect on the date of injury. It is computed on October

1 of each year and applies for the next twelve months. For injuries between October 1, 2007 and September 30, 2008, the maximum rate is $1,043.54.

EXAMPLE: Hank Taft is injured on September 1, 2008. His average weekly wage is $600. His compensation rate is $360.

EXAMPLE: Monica Mason is also injured on September 1, 2008. Her average weekly wage is $2,000. Her compensation rate is the maximum, $1,043.54.

Computing average wages. An employee's average weekly wage is computed by dividing his or her gross pay from the employer over the preceding twelve months by fifty-two. If more than two weeks was lost due to illness, injury, or inclement weather, gross pay is divided by the number of weeks worked.

When an employee's length of service is shorter than a year, gross earnings are divided by the number of weeks worked. If the employee only worked for a few days or weeks, the insurer can use the wages of another employee doing the same work over the previous year.

When an employee has a second job at the time of injury and is disabled from performing that job also, earnings from the second job are added to the earnings from the first job. Both jobs must be for insured employers.

EXAMPLE: Henry Beard has two jobs: one paying $600 per week and the other paying $200. If he is injured at either, and is unable to work, his compensation rate will be $480 (60 percent of $800).

Employer contributions to medical insurance and other benefit programs are not considered when computing wages. An exception applies if the worker's job is subject to the state prevailing wage laws.[241]

Dependents. If an employee's compensation rate is less than $150, $6 per week is added for each dependent.

Duration. Injured workers can collect TTI benefits for up to 156 weeks (three years if the period is continuous).

Permanent and Total Incapacity

Employees whose injuries permanently disable them from all work on the labor market are entitled to permanent and total (P&T) benefits for the rest of their lives. The weekly rate is 66 percent of average wages up to the applicable maximum. Cost-of-living allowances are added unless they reduce social security benefits.

EXAMPLE: Jerry Minter was paid temporary total incapacity benefits at the rate of $540 (60 percent of his average wage of $900). After three years, he won a claim for permanent and total incapacity. His rate increased to $600 (66 percent) and he became eligible for cost-of-living increases.

Partial Incapacity

Partial incapacity benefits are paid if a job injury reduces an employee's earning capacity but does not entirely prevent him from working. Examples include an employee who must change to a lower-paying occupation, stop working overtime, or work a reduced workweek. The payment rate is 60 percent of lost earning capacity.

EXAMPLE: Gordon Weiler, a construction worker earning $800 per week, was hurt in a fall. The injury totally disabled him for nine months during which time he received compensation at the rate of $480 per week (60 percent). Unable to return to his regular job, he took a sales position paying $500 per week. Since his wage loss is $300, the compensation insurer must pay him $180 per week (60 percent of $300).

NOTE: Partial incapacity benefits cannot exceed 75 percent of an employee's TTI rate. Using the example above, if Weiler earned $100 per week, his partial compensation rate would be capped at $360, 75 percent of $480.

Duration. An employee can receive partial incapacity benefits for up to 260 weeks (equivalent to five years) except that if an employee receives TTI benefits for 156 weeks, the maximum period of partial incapacity benefits is 208 weeks (four years).[242]

Medical Services

Insurers must pay for all reasonable and necessary medical services needed to treat job injuries and illnesses, including psychiatric counseling. Services must be preapproved. Travel expenses are included (the current rate is forty cents per mile).

Medical coverage includes chiropractic, massage, and acupuncture treatments that relieve pain, reduce dependence on medications, or help to restore function.

If an insurer accepts a case, a lump sum settlement does not affect its responsibility to provide future medical coverage.

Vocational Rehabilitation

Workers who cannot return to their regular jobs are entitled to vocational rehabilitation. Services may include instruction at a technical school or a college. If a DIA counselor recommends that a worker be retrained, the worker must cooperate or face a reduction of benefits.

Disfigurement

In addition to weekly benefits, insurers must pay cash awards if an injury causes permanent scarring of the face, neck, or hands. Payments are also due if a worker uses a cane or walks with a limp. Recommended payments ("Section 36 Guidelines") are listed on the DIA website. Employees can call the DIA Conciliation Unit for advice (617-727-4900, ext. 369).

Loss of Function

Loss-of-function benefits are due if an injury causes a permanent impairment of a body part or sense. An amputation is the extreme case. Payments depend on the body part involved and the percentage of function lost. Guidelines are on the DIA website.

> **EXAMPLE:** Warren Talbot suffered a 20 percent loss of leg function from a 2008 injury. Since the payment for loss of a leg is $40,698.06, Talbot is due $8,139.12.

Death Benefits

Spouses of workers who die of job injuries are entitled to benefits. The weekly rate is two-thirds of the deceased employee's average wage up to the maximum level. Burial expenses are reimbursed up to $4,000.

Death benefits are paid indefinitely if the widow or widower is not fully self-supporting. Otherwise, payments end when they reach 250 times the state average weekly wage in effect on the date of injury. If a widow or widower remarries, spousal benefits cease and children younger than 18 are paid $60 per week.

Double Compensation

Insurers must pay double compensation if an employer or supervisor causes an injury through serious and willful misconduct. An example is an assault on an employee. Double compensation is also payable if a minor is injured while performing duties that violate a child labor law. In either case the employer must reimburse the insurer for the extra amount.

PROCEDURES

Employees, employers, insurers, and the DIA must adhere to the following procedures.

Reporting Injury to Employer

Employees must report injuries to the employer or the insurance company "as soon as practicable."[243] This is usually the same or the next day. Late reports are not automatically disqualifying, but may prompt an insurer to dispute a claim.

Notice to Insurer

Employers must notify insurers and the DIA when an injury disables an employee for five or more calendar days. The report is due within seven days. A fine may be imposed for lateness.

> **EXAMPLE:** Rebecca Stowe was injured on March 6, 2008. Her fifth day of disability was March 10. Her employer must report the injury by March 17.

Paying Benefits

Insurers have fourteen calendar days from a report of injury to either commence payments or send a notice disputing an entitlement.

Claims

If an insurer contests an injury, the employee must file a DIA claim. Forms can be downloaded from the DIA website. If the employee hires an attorney, and a DIA judge approves the claim, the insurer must pay the attorney. Attorneys may not charge employees if claims are unsuccessful.

Conciliation. Within fifteen days of a claim, the DIA holds a conciliation meeting. A DIA staff member mediates between the employee and the insurer.

Conference. If the conciliation fails to resolve the matter, the case is scheduled for a conference before a DIA administrative judge. If compensation is ordered, the insurer must begin payments within fourteen days.

Hearing. If either party is dissatisfied with the results of a conference, it can request a hearing. If the case involves a medical issue, the party must submit a $450 fee to the DIA to pay for an impartial examiner. Hearings are usually held within three months.

SIX THINGS TO DO IF YOU GET HURT ON THE JOB

- Report promptly to management.

- Record the names of witnesses.

- If the pain is severe, go to a clinic or a hospital.

- Ask the nurse or doctor to note that the injury happened at work.

- Obtain copies of your records.

- Call the workers' compensation insurer to make sure it is aware of the injury.

Stopping Benefits

Insurers can require injured workers to attend examinations by so-called independent medical examiners (IMEs). If the IME says the employee can return to work, the insurer can begin termination procedures, which vary depending on how many days benefits have been paid.

Within the first 180 days. An insurer that begins benefits within 14 days can pay "without prejudice" for 180 days. During this period, the insurer can terminate benefits unilaterally if an IME certifies that the employee is no longer disabled or that the condition is not work-related. The employee can contest the action at the DIA.

After 180 days. After 180 days, the insurer must file a complaint at the DIA seeking permission to terminate or reduce benefits. Checks must be mailed until the case is heard by a judge.

Other reasons. Insurers can stop payments immediately if the employee returns to work and earns his or her former wages. If wages are reduced, the insurer must pay at the partial incapacity rate. Insurers can also stop benefits if the employee's doctor reports that the worker can return to his or her previous job and the employer offers reinstatement.

Lump-sum Settlement

A lump-sum settlement is an agreement between an employee and an insurer in which the insurer pays a sum of money and the claimant gives up his or her rights to compensation. Insurers frequently offer settlements for severe injuries. The employee can accept, reject, or attempt to negotiate a higher amount. The employer must approve the settlement amount.

RETURNING TO WORK

Three laws apply when an employee returns to work:
- The Family and Medical Leave Act (FMLA) requires employers to reinstate eligible employees to their original jobs or equivalent positions if the employee returns within twelve weeks and can perform his or her essential duties. See Chapter 4.
- The Massachusetts Workers' Compensation Act requires employers to grant recovered employees preferences over nonemployees for open positions for which the employee is qualified.[244]
- Injured workers are considered "qualified handicapped persons" under the Massachusetts Fair Employment Practices Act (FEPA) if they can perform the essential duties of an available position.[245] When necessary, employers must adjust schedules, modify assignments, or purchase special equipment to allow employees to return to work. See Chapter 11.

Questions *and* Answers

Lawsuit

Q: Can I sue my company if I contract cancer from chemicals at work?

A: No. Employers who provide workers' compensation coverage are immune from personal injury lawsuits by employees and their dependents. Supervisors enjoy similar protections.

Third party

Q: Are there any situations in which an injured worker can sue in civil court?

A: Yes. Workers can sue outside entities—for example, manufacturers of dangerous machinery or chemicals—if negligence on their part contributes to an injury. If the suit is successful, the employee must reimburse the workers' compensation insurer.

Course of treatment

Q: My doctor wants me to have an operation. If I decline, can the insurer stop my benefits?

A: Usually no. Injured workers can refuse medical procedures which carry risks or whose outcomes are doubtful.

Taxes

Q: Is workers' compensation taxable?

A: No.

Age 65

Q: Do compensation benefits stop at 65?

A: No, the compensation act does not contain an age cutoff.

Uninsured employer

Q: My employer does not carry compensation insurance. Am I out of luck?

A: No. A special DIA fund pays benefits to employees of uninsured employers. You may also sue your employer for negligence.

Undocumented worker

Q: Can an undocumented employee collect workers' compensation?

A: Yes. The DIA has ruled that undocumented employees are entitled to compensation benefits as if they were lawfully employed.[246]

Glossary

Accrued leave Leave earned by virtue of past service.

Affirmative action Effort by employer to increase numbers of women and minorities.

Arbitration Method of settling grievances between union and employer in which a neutral person, an arbitrator, is selected to resolve the dispute.

At-will employee Employee not covered by union or individual employment contract.

Authorization card Card that states a desire for union representation.

Bargaining unit Group of workers represented by a union

Collective bargaining agreement Contract between employer and union.

Compensatory time Time off in lieu of overtime pay.

Concerted activity Activity by two or more employees to improve wages or working conditions or activity by single employee on the authorization of others or to encourage group action.

Constructive discharge Resignation in response to intolerable conditions.

Disparate impact Job qualification or standard, neutral on its face, which disproportionally excludes women, minorities, or disabled individuals.

Disparate treatment Adverse action because of an individual's race, gender, or other protected status.

Essential functions Duties that are fundamental to a position.

Exempt employee Employee who, because of job duties and salary level, need not be paid overtime compensation.

Fitness-for-duty report Report from a health care provider certifying that an employee can return to duty.

Fixed workweek agreement Understanding that a salary is to cover a fixed number of hours.

Fluctuating workweek agreement Understanding that a salary covers straight time no matter how many hours are worked and that the overtime premium will be 50 percent of the regular rate.

Grievance Employee or union complaint alleging violation of the collective bargaining agreement, past practice, or state or federal law.

Hostile environment harassment Conduct that creates an intimidating, hostile, or humiliating work environment.

Intermittent leave Leave taken on a sporadic or occasional basis.

Lockout Employer order barring employees from entering facility.

Nonexempt employee Employee entitled to overtime compensation if hours exceed forty in a workweek.

Past practice Consistent way of doing things over an extended period.

Prevailing wage Minimum rate on public works projects.

Punitive damages Sum of money awarded to a plaintiff to punish the defendant and set an example for others.

Quid pro quo harassment Pressure on employee by manager or supervisor to engage in sexual activity.

Reasonable accommodation Change in equipment, schedule, duties, work rule applications, or other employment conditions that allows an employee to perform his or her essential job duties.

Regular rate Figure on which overtime compensation is calculated.

Service rate Minimum cash wage for tipped employees.

Show-up pay Payment due an employee who arrives as scheduled but is not provided with expected work.

Statute of limitations Deadline for filing a complaint or lawsuit.

Sunday law holiday Holiday for which a police permit is necessary for certain businesses to operate.

Unfair labor practice Violation by employer or union of obligations imposed by the National Labor Relations Act.

Vesting Years of employment necessary to secure a nonforfeitable right to employer pension contributions.

Weingarten right Right of employee to request union representation if interrogated by a supervisor.

Whistleblower Employee who reports wrongdoing.

Appendix I

Government Agencies

Criminal History Systems Board (CHSB)

200 Arlington St., Suite 2200
Chelsea, MA 02150
617-660-4613

Equal Employment Opportunity Commission (EEOC)

www.eeoc.gov

John F. Kennedy Federal
  Building
475 Government Center
Boston, MA 02203
800-669-4000

Fair Labor Division of the Massachusetts Attorney General

www.ago.state.ma.us
  (click Wage and Hour)

100 Cambridge St., 12th Floor
Boston, MA 02108
617-727-3465

105 William St.
New Bedford, MA 02740
508-990-9700

1350 Main St.
Springfield, MA 01103
413-784-1128

One Exchange Pl.
Worcester, MA 01608
508-792-7600

Federal Labor Relations Authority (FLRA)

www.flra.gov

10 Causeway St., Rm. 1017
Boston, MA 02222
617-565-7280

Federal Mediation and Conciliation Service (FMCS)

www.fmcs.gov

2100 K St. NW
Washington, DC 20427
202-653-5300

Massachusetts Commission Against Discrimination (MCAD)

www.state.ma.us/mcad

One Ashburton Pl., Rm. 601
Boston, MA 02108
617-994-6000

436 Dwight St., Rm. 220
Springfield, MA 01103
413-739-2145

455 Main St., Room 100
Worccester, MA 01608
508-799-8010

Massachusetts Department of Industrial Accidents (DIA)

www.mass.gov/dia

600 Washington St., 7th Floor
Boston, MA 02111
617-727-4900

1 Father Devalles Blvd.
Fall River, MA 02723
508-676-3406

160 Winthrop Ave.
Lawrence, MA 01843
978-683-6420

436 Dwight St.
Springfield, MA 01103
413-784-1133

340 Main St., Suite 370
Worcester, MA 01608
508-753-2072

Massachusetts Division of Labor Relations (DLR)

www.mass.gov/dlr

19 Staniford St., 1st Floor
Boston, MA 02114
617-626-7132

Massachusetts Division of Occupational Safety (DOS)

www.mass.gov/dos

19 Staniford St.
Boston, MA 02114
617-626-6975

Massachusetts Division of Unemployment Assistance (DUA)

www.mass.gov/dua

Charles F. Hurley Building
Government Center
19 Staniford St.
Boston, MA 02114
617-626-6560

Massachusetts Tobacco Control Program

250 Washington St., 4th Floor
Boston, MA 02108
617-624-5900

National Institute for Occupational Safety and Health (NIOSH)

www.cdc.gov/niosh

New England Field Office
P.O. Box 87040
South Dartmouth, MA 02748
508-997-6126

National Labor Relations Board (NLRB)

www.nlrb.gov

Thomas P. O'Neil Federal Bldg.
10 Causeway St., Suite 601
Boston, MA 02222
617-565-6700

Occupational Safety and Health Administration (OSHA)

www.osha.gov

North Boston Area Office
Valley Office Park 13 Branch St.
Methuen, Massachusetts 01844
617-565-8110

South Boston Area Office
639 Granite St., 4th Floor
Braintree, Massachusetts 02184
617-565-6924

Springfield Area Office
1441 Main St., Rm. 550
Springfield, Massachusetts 01103
413-785-0123

Office of Federal Contract Compliance Programs (OFCCP)

www.dol.gov/esa/ofccp

John F. Kennedy Federal
Building, Rm. E-235
Boston, MA 02203
617-624-6780

Office of Labor-Management Standards (OLMS)

www.dol.gov/esa/olms_org.htm

JFK Federal Bldg, Rm E-365
Boston, MA 02203
617-624-6690

Office of Special Counsel for Immigration-Related Unfair Employment Practices (OSC)

www.usdoj.gov/crt/osc

P.O. Box 27728
Washington D.C. 20038
800-255-7688

Pension and Welfare Benefits Administration (PWBA)

www.dol.gov/ebsa

J.W. McCormack POCH
Building
Boston, MA 02109
617-223-9837

U.S. Department of Labor (DOL)

www.dol.gov

Regional Office
One Congress St., 11th Floor
Boston, MA 02114
617-565-2072

Wage and Hour Division (U.S. Department of Labor)

www.dol.gov/esa/whd

JFK Building, Rm. 525
Boston, MA 02203
617-624-6700

1441 Main St., Rm. 420
Springfield, MA 01103
413-785-0354

17 Broadway, Rm. 308
Taunton, MA 02780
508-821-9106

Veteran's Employment and Training Service (VETS)

www.dol.gov/vets

One Congress St.
Boston, MA 02114
617-565-2081

Appendix II
Advocacy Organizations

ADP Worker Center/ Casa Obrera
130 Union St.
Springfield, MA 01105
413-739-7233

Association of Haitian Women
www.afab-kafanm.org
330 Fuller St.
Dorchester, MA 02124
617-287-0096

Boston Workers Alliance
www.bostonworkersalliance.org
51 Roxbury St.
Boston, MA 02119
617-427-8108

Brazilian Immigrant Center
www.braziliancenter.org
10 Harvard Ave.
Allston, MA 02134
617-783-8001

Brazilian Workers Center
www.ctbboston.org
68 Central St.
East Boston, MA 02128
617-569-0006

Casa Latina
www.casalatinainc.org
140 Pine St.
Florence, MA 01062
413-586-1569

Centro Presente

www.cpresente.org

54 Essex St.
Cambridge, MA 02139
617-497-9080

Chelsea Collaborative

www.chelseacollab.org

300 Broadway St.
Chelsea, MA 02150
617-869-6080

Chinese Progressive Association Workers Center

www.cpaboston.org/mission.html

33 Harrison Ave.
Boston, MA 02111
617-357-4499

City Life/Vida Urbana

www.clvu.org/node/72

P.O. Box 17
Jamaica Plain, MA 02130
617-524-3541

American Civil Liberties Union of Massachusetts

www.aclu-mass.org

211 Congress Street 3rd Floor
Boston, MA 02110
617-482-3170

Disability Law Center

www.dlc-ma.org

11 Beacon St.
Boston, MA 02108
617-723-8455

Gay and Lesbian Advocates and Defenders

www.glad.org

30 Winter St.
Boston, MA 02108
617-426-1350

East Boston Ecumenical Community Council

www.ebecc.org

50 Meridian St.
East Boston, MA 02128
617-567-2750

Foundation for Fair Contracting

www.ffcm.org

11 Beacon St.
Boston, MA 02108
617-248-8864

Greater Boston Labor Council

www.gbclc.com

8 Beacon St.
Boston, MA 02110
617-723-2370

Greater Boston Legal Services

www.gbls.org

197 Friend St.
Boston, MA 02114
617-371-1234

Irish Immigration Center

www.iicenter.org

59 Temple Pl.
Boston, MA 02111
617-542-7654

Jobs with Justice

www.massjwj.net

3353 Washington St.
Jamaica Plain, MA 02130
617-525-8778

640 Page Blvd.
Springfield, MA 01104
413-731-0760

Labor Guild of Boston

www.laborguild.com

85 Commercial St.
Weymouth, MA 01188
781-340-7887

Lawyers Committee for Civil Rights Under Law

www.lawyerscommittee.org

294 Washington St.
Boston, MA 02108
617-482-1145

Legal Advocacy and Resource Center

www.larcma.org

197 Friend Street, 9th Floor
Boston, MA 02114
800-342-5297

Massachusetts AFL-CIO

www.massaflcio.org

389 Main St.
Malden, MA 02148
781-324-8230

Massachusetts Bar Association

www.massbar.org

20 West St.
Boston, MA 02111
617-338-0500

Massachusetts Coalition for Occupational Safety and Health

www.masscosh.org

42 Charles St.
Dorchester, MA 02122
617-825-7233

458 Bridge St.
Springfield, MA 01103
413-731-0760

Massachusetts Senior Action Council

www.masssenioraction.org

565 Warren St.
Boston, MA 02121
617-442-3330

Merrimack Valley Labor Council

www.mvclc.org

169 Merrimack St.
Lowell, MA 01852
978-441-1939

Merrimack Valley Project Worker Center

www.merrimackvalleyproject.org

1045 Essex St.
Lawrence, MA 01840
978-686-0650

National Employment Lawyers Association

www.nela.org

50 Congress St.
Boston, MA 02100
617-720-2400

National Lawyers Guild

www.nlgmass.org

14 Beacon St.
Boston, MA 02108
617-227-7335

National Organization of Women

www.now.org

1105 Commonwealth Ave.
Allston, MA 02115
617-254-9130

North Shore Labor Council

www.nslaborcouncil.org

112 Exchange St.
Lynn, MA 01901
781-595-2538

Pioneer Valley Labor Council

640 Page Blvd.
Springfield, MA
413-732-7970

Union of Minority Neighborhoods

www.unionofminorityneighborhoods.
org

83 Highland St.
Roxbury, MA 02109
617-541-4111

Worcester Interfaith Workers Center

111 Park St.
Worcester, MA
508-754-5001

Notes

The notes include laws, regulations, court decisions and other information. The most common abbreviations are:

Laws

M.G.L.   Massachusetts General Laws
U.S.C.   United States Code

EXAMPLES: M.G.L. ch. 149, §148 means section 148 of Chapter 149 of the Massachusetts General Laws. 29 U.S.C. §206 means section 206 of Title 29 of the U.S. Code.

Regulations

CMR   Code of Massachusetts Regulations
CFR   Code of Federal Regulations

EXAMPLE: 29 CFR §778 means section 778 of Title 29 of the Code of Federal Regulations.

Court Decisions

Mass.   Massachusetts Supreme Judicial Court
Mass.App.Ct.   Massachusetts Appeals Court
U.S.   United States Supreme Court
F.2d or F.3d   United States Circuit Court
F.Supp.   United States District Court

EXAMPLE: Jancey v. School Committee of Everett, 421 Mass. 482 (1995) means that the case is in volume 421 of Massachusetts Reports beginning on page 482. The case was decided in 1995.

1. M.G.L. ch.149, §148.

2. Hospital employees must request to be paid weekly. M.G.L. ch.149, §148 (paragraph 4).

3. **NOTE:** Coverage of state employees is limited to mechanics, workmen, laborers, and employees in charitable and penal institutions.

4. Independent contractors are defined in M.G.L. ch.149, §148B. *See,* infra, p. 27.

5. **NOTE:** Criminal penalties include a fine of up to $25,000 and a jail sentence of up to one year. **FURTHER NOTE:** Public officials cannot be held responsible if prevented from performing their duties through no fault of their own. M.G.L. ch.149, §148 (paragraph 5).

6. *See* Caswell v. Ferrara & Sons, Inc., 2002 WL 31986854 (D.Mass. 2002) (applying a principle known as "federal preemption"). **NOTE:** Where the amount due does not require contract interpretation, unionized employees may sue for penalties without taking the matter through their grievance and arbitration procedure. Newton v. Comm'r of Dep't of Youth Servs., 62 Mass.App.Ct. 343, 347 (2004).

7. M.G.L. ch.149, §148 (paragraph 5).

8. M.G.L. ch.149, §148 (paragraph 3). *See* Wiedmann v. The Bradford Group, Inc., 444 Mass. 698, 708–709 (2005).

9. M.G.L. ch.149, §148 (paragraphs 1 and 6).

10. M.G.L. ch.149, §148 (paragraph 1). *See* Pride Auto Group v. Office of the Attorney General, DALA (Division of Administrative Law Appeals) LB-04-573 (2007) (company policy that employees who resign or are terminated are not entitled to accrued vacation time, illegal special agreement).

11. M.G.L. ch.149, §150 (sentence 2).

12. Penalties for Wage Act violations are set forth in M.G.L. ch.149, §27C.

13. 29 U.S.C. §207(a)(1); M.G.L. ch.151, §1A. **NOTE:** Overtime pay for state employees is also regulated by M.G.L. ch.149, §30B, which mandates time-and-a-half wages for hours in excess of eight in a day. Several exceptions apply.

14. **NOTE:** An exception applies to hospitals and nursing homes which, with the agreement of employees, may pay time-and-one-half for hours in excess of eighty in a 14-day period on the condition that overtime rates are paid for time worked in excess of eight in a day. 29 U.S.C. §207(j).

15. *See* M.G.L. ch.151, §1A(8). **NOTE:** Commercial vehicles must be rated as safe to operate at a weight exceeding 10,001 pounds or more inclusive of the vehicle's load. *See* 49 CFR §390.5.

16. M.G.L. ch.151, §15 (final sentence). **NOTE:** This law is not restricted to nonexempt employees.

17. **NOTE:** An assistant manager who only exercises supervision in a

manager's absence does not meet this test.

18. *See* 29 U.S.C. §213(a)(17). **NOTE:** The Massachusetts overtime act does not include a computer-worker exemption: employers must pay overtime unless employees meet the administrative or professional exemption tests. This is not a given. *See* Pezzillo v. General Telephone and Electronics Information Systems, Inc., 414 F.Supp. 1257, 1265-1269 (D. Tenn. 1976) (no administrative exemption during periods when programming duties are routine).

19. **NOTE:** An exemption applies to workers in retail stores or other service establishments (including automobile repair) who (1) are paid a wage that exceeds one-and-a-half-times the minimum wage and (2) receive more than half their compensation in the form of commissions. 29 U.S.C. §207(i). **FURTHER NOTE:** When an employee is covered only by Massachusetts law, commission, bonus, and incentive pay is excluded in computing the regular rate. M.G.L. ch.151, §1A (second sentence).

20. *See* Minimum Wage Program Frequently Asked Questions (Question 8), Division of Occupational Safety (www.mass.gov/dos/mw/mw_faq.htm) ("If an employee is a non-exempt employee, meaning an employee who is due overtime, the employer may not award compensatory time in place of paying overtime compensation.").

21. *See* 29 U.S.C. §207(o)(5).

22. *See* 29 CFR §778.113(a).

23. *See* 29 CFR §785.7.

24. 29 CFR §§785.11-13. *See* Chao v. Gotham Registry, Inc., 514 F.3d 280 (2nd Cir. 2008) (employer must pay overtime rate for hours in excess of forty even if work is in violation of company policies).

25. *See* 29 CFR §§785.11 and 12; Warren v. Edgeco, Inc., 8 Mass.App.Ct. 171, 174-175 (1979).

26. *See* 29 CFR §785.19(a) and 29 CFR §553.223(b). **NOTE:** The courts disagree as to whether these rules are valid for employees whose only duties are to remain on call during lunch periods. *Compare* Kohlheim v. Glynn County, Ga., 915 F.2d 1473, 1477 (11th Cir. 1990) (time compensable) *with* Henson v. Pulaski County Sheriff Dept., 6 F.3d 531, 534–536 (8th Cir. 1993) (time not compensable).

27. *See* DOS Opinion Letter MW 2003–008 (August 5, 2003) (enforcing Massachusetts law). **NOTE:** The U.S. Department of Labor takes a different position in enforcing the FLSA. *See* 29 CFR §785.19(b).

28. **NOTE:** Transportation expenses must be reimbursed. *See* 455 CMR §2.03(4)(b).

29. **NOTE:** An exception may apply if an employee carries out work activities prior to leaving home. *See* Dooley v. Liberty Mutual Ins. Co., 307 F.Supp.2d 234, 242 (D.Mass. 2004) (checking email and voice mail, preparing computers, and returning telephone calls, part of appraisers' regular work). Moreover, if an employee with a fixed work location is required to report to another worksite, any extra travel time must be compensated and expenses must be reimbursed.

455 CMR §2.03(4)(a).

30. M.G.L. ch.149, §148B (amended 2004). **NOTE:** The §148B tests are used to determine employee status under the Wage Act, the Minimum Wage Act, the Overtime Act, the prevailing wage laws, and other laws in Chapters 149 and 151 of the Massachusetts General Laws. Similar tests apply under the unemployment insurance statute, except that a contractor can satisfy the second requirement by working away from the employer's premises. *See* M.G.L. ch.151A, §2.

31. *See* M.G.L. ch.149, §148B(d). **NOTE:** An employer may be able to escape overtime liability if it can prove that an employee's higher salary as an independent contractor exceeds the unpaid overtime. *See* Somers v. Convergical Access, Inc., 23 Mass.L.Rptr. 511 (Middlesex Super. Ct. 2008).

32. M.G.L. ch.149, §148B(d). **NOTE:** The statute does not prevent an employer from subcontracting work to legitimate third-party employers or S corporations. Nor does it affect contracts with temporary help agencies.

33. *See* 455 CMR §2.03(3).

34. 29 CFR §785.42. **NOTE:** Massachusetts does not have a similar exemption. *See* 455 CMR 2.01 (defining "working time" as all time, with the exception of meal breaks, during which employees are required to be on premises).

35. **NOTE:** Lawsuits can be filed up to three years after a willful violation.

36. *Compare* M.G.L. ch.151, §1 *with* 29 U.S.C. §206(a)(1) (amended 2007). **NOTE:** The state standard was raised to $8 on January 1, 2008.

37. *See* Grenier v. Town of Hubbardston, 7 Mass.App.Ct. 911, rescript (1979) (state minimum wage law does not apply to government agencies because legislature did not express intention to apply law to the public sector). **NOTE:** Jancey v. School Committee of Everett, 421 Mass. 482, 499 (1995) can be read to suggest that state labor laws apply to public agencies unless the legislature has expressly indicated otherwise. Nonetheless, the Division of Occupational Safety has concluded that under both *Grenier* and *Jancey*, the state minimum wage law does not apply to public agencies. Division of Occupational Safety Opinion Letter MW-2002-001 (January 11, 2002). **FURTHER NOTE:** Agricultural employees are covered by the FLSA's minimum wage requirement unless they are subject to one of the act's exclusions, for example, range employees or employees on farms employing small numbers of workers. Workers exempt from the FLSA come under the state agricultural minimum wage of $1.60 per hour. M.G.L. ch.151, §2A.

38. 455 CMR §2.02(2)(b). **NOTE:** Under federal rules, service rates may not be applied to employees who receive less than $30 per month in tips (state law is $20). **FURTHER NOTE:** The Boston district office of the Department of Labor currently computes the overtime rate for tipped employees by multiplying 1.5 times the state minimum wage and deducting the state tip credit of $5.37.

The result is a minimum cash rate of $6.63. In other states, DOL deducts the federal tip credit. It is anticipated that the latter method, which results in a cash rate of $7.58 per hour as of July 24, 2008, and $6.88 as of July 24, 2009, will eventually be applied in Massachusetts.

39. M.G.L. ch.151, §7 (paragraph 3, last sentence).

40. **NOTE:** State law is ambiguous about when employers must pay credit card tips. On the one hand employers must turn over tips by the end of the same business day; on the other, payments can be made up to six days after the end of the applicable pay period. *See* M.G.L. ch.149, §152A(e). **FURTHER NOTE:** DOL permits employers to subtract fees charged by credit card companies to process card payments. Wage and Hour Opinion Letter WH-410 (March 28, 1977). There is no Massachusetts ruling on the practice.

41. **NOTE:** For enforcement purposes, DOL considers a net loss of up to 15 percent to meet this test. A higher percentage must be justified by practices in the locality.

42. M.G.L. ch.149, §152A(e).

43. M.G.L. ch.149, §§148A and 150 (employees can sue for triple damages plus legal fees). *See* Smith v. Winter Place LLC, 447 Mass. 363, 367-368 (2006).

44. 455 CMR §2.04(1)(b).

45. 455 CMR §2.04(1)(c). **NOTE:** Tip pools of service workers outside of the food and beverage industry, for example among hotel cleaning staff, are also barred from making distributions to persons with managerial responsibilities. *Id.*

46. *See* DOL Wage and Hour Division Fact Sheet #16: Deductions From Wages for Uniforms and Other Facilities Under the Fair Labor Standards Act (FLSA). **NOTE:** Minimum wage employees may not be asked for a uniform deposit unless the employer obtains a license from the Director of Labor and Workforce Development. 455 CMR §2.04(2)(b).

47. 455 CMR §2.03(1). **NOTE:** The regulation would appear to apply to an emplolyee who reports to work as scheduled but is immediately suspended or discharged. **FURTHER NOTE:** The regulation does not apply to charitable organizations. *Id.*

48. M.G.L. ch.149, §§26-27; 40 U.S.C. §§3142-3148.

49. **NOTE:** The attorney general can prosecute, assess civil penalties, order restitution, halt work on projects, and seek orders debarring contractors from government contracts. Workers paid improper wages can sue for triple damages. *See* M.G.L. ch.149, §27C.

50. Martino v. Mich. Window Cleaning Co., 327 U.S. 173, 178 (1946).

51. *See* 29 U.S.C. §§207(h)(2) and 207(e)(5).

52. **NOTE:** A bill barring mandatory overtime for hospital nurses passed the Massachusetts House of Representatives on May 22, 2008.

53. M.G.L. ch.208, §36A(5).

54. 29 CFR §553.230(b). **NOTE:** Fire protection agencies do not have to pay overtime unless a firefighter's hours exceed 53 in a 7-day

period, 212 in a 28-day period, or a proportionate number for a period between 7 and 28 days. 29 CFR §553.230(a).

55. *See* Division of Occupational Safety, Opinion Letter MW 2002-020 (July 19, 2002).

56. M.G.L. ch.149, §100 ("No person shall be required to work for more than six hours during a calendar day without an interval of at least thirty minutes for a meal.").

57. *See* Division of Occupational Safety Opinion Letter MW 2003–008. (August 5, 2003).

58. *See* M.G.L. ch.149, §101.

59. *See* M.G.L ch.149, §§148A and 150 (providing for civil sanctions and remedies against employers who retaliate against Chapter 149 complainants).

60. M.G.L. ch.149, §103 (punishable by a fine of $50 to $200).

61. M.G.L. ch.149, §139 (punishable by a fine of $5 to $20).

62. 29 CFR §1910.141(c).

63. 29 CFR §1926.51(c).

64. OSHA Interpretive Memorandum, April 6, 1998.

65. M.G.L. ch.149, §113.

66. 29 CFR §1910.151(b).

67. M.G.L. ch.149, §106. *See also* 29 CFR §1910.141(b)(1) (general industry); 29 CFR §1926.51(a) (construction).

68. M.G.L. ch.136, §7. Among the exemptions are retail trade, transportation, banking, baking, law, and health care. *See* M.G.L. ch.136, §6.

69. M.G.L. ch.136, §6(50) (paragraph 2) (refusal to work may not be grounds for dismissal, reduc-

tion in hours, discrimination, or other penalty).

70. *Id.* **NOTE:** A retail employee who works forty hours during the week and eight hours on Sunday need only be paid overtime rates for eight hours.

71. M.G.L. ch.149, §45 (punishable by a fine of up to $1,500).

72. M.G.L. ch.136, §§13 and 16.

73. M.G.L. ch.136, §§13 and 16. Fine is $1,000.

74. M.G.L. ch.149, §48 (day of rest must include twenty-four consecutive hours without labor). Penalty is a $300 fine. **NOTE:** An employee who is discharged for refusing to work more than six consecutive days can sue under M.G.L. ch.149, §148A. *See* Bujold v. EMC Corp., 23 Mass.L.Rptr. 347 (Suffolk Sup. Ct. 2007). **FURTHER NOTE:** Employers must post lists of employees working on Sundays and the day of rest assigned. M.G.L. ch.149, §51.

75. M.G.L. ch.149, §47. Punishable by a fine of up to $300.

76. M.G.L. ch.148, §§ 49 and 50.

77. M.G.L. ch.151B, §4(1A).

78. 38 U.S.C. §4301 et seq.

79. **NOTE:** An employer need not reinstate a returning service member if reemployment is unreasonable, impossible, or would cause an undue hardship. 38 U.S.C. §4312(d)(1).

80. M.G.L. ch.149, §188(b). **NOTE:** This portion of the law is likely to face a legal challenge contending that it is "pre-empted" by the federal ERISA law.

81. 114.5 CMR §16.03.

82. M.G.L. ch.175, §110(0) (not including stand-alone dental plans).

83. 29 U.S.C. §§1161-1168 (Consolidated Omnibus Budget Reconciliation Act). **NOTE:** Employees can continue for up to twenty-nine months in the case of disability. **FURTHER NOTE:** COBRA does not apply to employees terminated for gross misconduct.

84. M.G.L. ch.176J, §9.

85. M.G.L. ch.175, §110D.

86. M.G.L. ch.175, §110*I* and M.G.L. ch.176G, §5A. **NOTE:** Spousal coverage can end before remarriage if provided by the divorce judgement. *Id.* **FURTHER NOTE:** Employer self-funded plans may not be governed by these statutes. *See* Bergin v. Wausau Ins. Companies, 863 F.Supp. 34 (D.Mass. 1994).

87. M.G.L. ch.270, §22 (does not apply to home offices, private clubs, hotel smoking rooms, smoking bars, or retail tobacco stores).

88. 29 U.S.C. §2101 et seq. **NOTE:** The period to measure covered job losses is extended to ninety days in the case of connected lay-offs or closings.

89. M.G.L. ch.175, §110D and §110G; ch.176A, §8D; ch.176B, §6A; ch.176G, §4A. **NOTE:** A plant closing is defined as a permanent cessation or reduction of business which causes the separation of at least 90 percent of the employees of the facility. M.G.L. ch.151A, §71A; a partial closing is a cessation which affects a "significant number" of employees. *Id.*

90. 29 U.S.C. §1001 et seq. (Employee Retirement Income Security Act).

91. M.G.L. ch.149, §187.

92. 18 U.S.C. §1514A.

93. **NOTE:** OSHA has been given jurisdiction over the anti-retaliation provisions of many federal whistleblower laws, presumably because of the agency's experience in handling investigations under the OSH Act.

94. M.G.L. ch.149, §185.

95. 31 U.S.C. §§3729-3733; M.G.L. ch.12, §§5A-5O.

96. York v. Zurich Scudder Investments, Inc., 66 Mass.App.Ct. 610, 614 (2006). **NOTE:** Employers are not free to renege on definite promises, such as clear guarantees in personnel manuals. *See* LeMaitre v. Massachusetts Turnpike Authority, 70 Mass.App.Ct. 634 (2007) (payments for unused sick leave).

97. *See* Fortune v. National Cash Register Co., 373 Mass. 96 (1977) (recognizing an implied covenant of good faith and fair dealing).

98. *See* DeRose v. Putnam Management Co., Inc., 398 Mass. 205 (1986) (refusal to give false testimony about another employee); Flesner v. Technical Communications Corp., 410 Mass. 805, 810 (1991) (assisting governmental investigation into illegal conduct); D'Alessandro v. Nipmuc, Inc., 22 Mass.L.Rptr. 1 (Middlesex Sup.Ct. 2007) (consulting an attorney). **NOTE:** Reporting fellow employees or supervisors who violate internal company policies or rules is apparently not shielded by the public policy exception.

99. *See* King v. Driscoll, 418 Mass. 576, 583 (1994).

100. M.G.L. ch.149, §74.

101. **NOTE:** M.G.L. ch.149, §56 lists establishments subject to the nine-hour rule. Although the list is comprehensive, covering manufacturing, mechanical, mercantile, office, amusement, domestic service, and other work, not all places of employment are included.For example, there is no reference to daycare operations or camps. The statute also makes limited exceptions to the 48-hours-per-week rule.

102. M.G.L. ch.268, §14B.

103. M.G.L. ch.234A, §61. Penalties include a fine of up to $5,000. Employees may sue for triple damages, legal fees, and injunctive relief. *See also* M.G.L. ch.268, §14A (illegal to discharge person because of service as a state juror) and 28 U.S.C. §1875 (same for federal jury service).

104. M.G.L. ch.151B, §4(9) (enforced by the Massachusetts Commission Against Discrimination).

105. MCAD Fact Sheet: Discrimination on the Basis of Criminal Record; M.G.L. ch.151B, §4(9) (paragraph 2). *See* Kraft v. Police Commissioner of Boston, 410 Mass. 155, 157 (1991) ("The commissioner had no authority to discharge Kraft for giving false answers to questions that the commissioner under law had no right to ask...").

106. M.G.L. ch.276, §100A (paragraph 5). **NOTE:** Employers may not ask applicants or employees for copies of their criminal records. *See* M.G.L. ch.6, §172 (paragraph 5, sentence 3).

107. M.G.L. ch.6, §172.

108. *See* M.G.L. ch.71, §38R. **NOTE:**
Policies that deny employment because of arrest or conviction histories may run afoul of the bar on race discrimination.

109. 42 U.S.C. §12112(d)(2) (applicable to employers with fifteen or more employees); M.G.L. ch.151B, §4(16) (six or more employees). **NOTE:** Applicants can be invited to self-identify themselves as disabled for purposes of receiving affirmative action benefits. MCAD Guidelines: Employment Discrimination on the Basis of Handicap §IVE.

110. *See* MCAD Guidelines: Employment Discrimination on the Basis of Handicap §IVB.

111. M.G.L. ch.151B, §4(19)(a)(5). **NOTE:** Employer requests for genetic information are also prohibited by the federal Genetic Information Nondiscrimination Act of 2008 (GINA).

112. 42 U.S.C. §12112(d)(4)(A) ("A covered entity shall not require a medical examination ... unless such examination or inquiry is shown to be job-related and consistent with business necessity."). **NOTE:** If the employer assigns a physician, it must provide the employee with a copy of the report upon request. *See* M.G.L. ch.149, §19A.

113. *See* EEOC Enforcement Guidance: Disability-Related Inquiries and Medical Examinations of Employees Under the Americans with Disabilities Act (ADA).

114. **NOTE:** Employers may conduct periodic medical examinations of employees in public safety positions if they are narrowly tailored to address specific job-related concerns. EEOC Enforcement Guidance on Disability-Related

Inquiries and Medical Examinations of Employees Under the Americans with Disabilities Act (ADA), Question 18.

115. *See* 29 CFR §1630.14(c) and 42 U.S.C. §12201(c).

116. M.G.L. ch.214, §1B.

117. Webster v. Motorola, Inc., 418 Mass. 425, 430-434 (1994).

118. Guiney v. Police Commissioner of Boston, 411 Mass. 328 (1991). *But see* Bennett v. Massachusetts Bay Transp. Authority, 8 Mass.L. Rptr. 201 (Suffolk Sup. Ct. 1998) (random testing of train operators does not violate Article 14 where extensive evidence in the record suggests the prevalence of illegal drug use by employees whose bad judgment can cause catastrophic accidents). *See also* Lanier v. City of Woodburn, 518 F.3d 1147 (9th Cir. 2008) (pre-employment drug testing unconstitutional).

119. *See, e.g.,* 49 CFR §382.305 (commercial motor vehicle operators).

120. M.G.L. ch.111, §70F (sentence 2).

121. M.G.L. ch.151B, §4(19)(a)(3). **NOTE:** Discrimination based on genetic information is also prohibited by the Genetic Information Nondiscrimination Act of 2008 (GINA).

122. M.G.L. ch.149, §19B. **NOTE:** Employment applications must contain the following notice: "It is unlawful in Massachusetts to require or administer a lie detector test as a condition of employment or continued employment. An employer who violates this law shall be subject to criminal penalties and civil liability." *Id.*

123. *See* Foley v. Polaroid Corp., 400 Mass. 82, 92 (1987).

124. M.G.L. ch.272, §99.

125. M.G.L. ch.149, §52C. Enforcement is by the Fair Labor Division. **NOTE:** Employees can also request records of their work hours. M.G.L. ch.151, §15.

126. **NOTE:** The MPRA does not authorize copying fees.

127. 29 U.S.C. §157 (not applicable to managerial or supervisory employees). Public employees enjoy similar rights under M.G.L. ch.150E, §2 enforced by the Division of Labor Relations (DLR).

128. *See* Timekeeping Systems, Inc., 323 NLRB 244 (1997). **NOTE:** The NLRA does not apply to an employee who individually complains to supervision about conditions of work peculiar to the employee.

129. Churchill's Restaurant, 276 NLRB 775, 777 (1985); Groves Truck & Trailer, 281 NLRB 1194, 1194-1195 (1986). **NOTE:** Abusive or obscene conduct can forfeit statutory protections. *See* Media General Operations, Inc. v. NLRB, 394 F.3d 207, 211 (4th Cir. 2005).

130. *See* Guardsmark, LLC v. NLRB, 475 F.3d 369 (D.C. Cir. 2007). **NOTE:** Otherwise illegal rules may survive challenge if the employer clearly explains to employees that they are not intended to discourage organizing or other activities protected by the National Labor Relations Act.

131. **NOTE:** Rules forbidding oral solicitations solely during "working time," or the distribution of literature in "work areas" may be found to be lawful if they are applied equally to distributing flyers for community events, asking for charitable donations, and

taking part in similar activities. No-solicitation rules may also be lawful in the retail and gambling industries in areas frequented by customers.

132. **NOTE:** Employers can ban or limit badges or other insignia in "special circumstances" in locations where special circumstances apply, such as work areas where buttons are likely to interfere with production, operations, or safety. Examples may include patient care areas in hospitals and selling floors in retail stores. Workers who wear uniforms while dealing with the public may be restricted from wearing large or controversial buttons.

133. *See* 42 U.S.C. §§2000e(j) and 2000e-2(a)(1). *See also* M.G.L. ch.151B, §4(1A) (unlawful to "impose upon an individual as a condition of obtaining or retaining employment any terms or conditions, compliance with which would require such individual to violate, or forego the practice of, his creed or religion....").

134. *See* 15 U.S.C. §§1681a(d)(2)(D) and 1681a(x).

135. Moran v. Dunphy, 177 Mass. 485, 487 (1901).

136. **NOTE:** Police officers and fire-fighters hired after 1988 may be discharged if they smoke on or off the job. M.G.L. ch.41, §101A.

137. *See* Rankin v. McPherson, 483 U.S. 378 (1987).

138. Conn. Gen. Statutes §31-51q. *See* Cotto v. United Technologies Corp., 251 Conn. 1, 16 (1999) ("Section 31-51q extends protection of rights of free speech under the federal and the state constitutions to employees in the private

workplace.").

139. 29 U.S.C. §2601 et seq.

140. M.G.L. ch.149, §52D.

141. 29 CFR §825.302(c).

142. 29 CFR §§825.305(d).

143. 29 CFR §825.113(c). **NOTE:** In the First Circuit, an adult child's disability does not have to be permanent or long lasting to justify parental leave. *See* Navarro v. Pfizer Corp., 261 F.3d 90 (1st Cir. 2001) (pregnant child ordered to bed rest).

144. **NOTE:** An exception applies if the employee stands "in loco parentis" to his or her grandchild or was raised by a grandparent. 29 CFR §825.113(c)(3).

145. 29 CFR §825.202.

146. 29 CFR §825.207(e). **NOTE:** Under current policy, employees can draw on vacation or personal days even if company rules would normally preclude such benefits. In 2008, DOL announced proposed modifications to this policy.

147. *See* Brotherhood of Maintenance of Way Employees v. CSX Transportation, Inc., 2005 WL 3597700 *9 (N.D. Ill 2005) ("The FMLA does not allow employers to violate pre-existing contractual obligations. If CBA provisions grant employees the right to determine when, or in what manner, they utilize certain types of paid vacation and personal leave, those CBA provisions prevent employers from substituting such leave for FMLA leave."), aff'd, 478 F.3d 814 (7th Cir. 2007).

148. *See* 29 U.S.C. §2614(a)(4). **NOTE:** Medical examinations may be scheduled after an emplyee returns to work.

149. 29 CFR §825.216(c).

150. M.G.L. ch.149, §52D(b)(1).

151. M.G.L. ch.149, §52D(b)(2). **NOTE:** The SNLA does not define the term "routine," generating the possibility that a court or arbitrator may deem some medical appointments as nonqualifying.

152. M.G.L. ch.149, §52D(a).

153. *See* 940 CMR §20.04. **NOTE:** The request may not be unreasonable or burdensome. *Id.*

154. **NOTE:** In the event of discharge an employee can sue for triple back pay.

155. M.G.L. ch.149, §105D. **NOTE:** Although §105D refers only to female employees, the Massachusetts Commission Against Discrimination has announced that it will be applying the law to both men and women (*Massachusetts Lawyers Weekly*, June 5, 2008). **FURTHER NOTE:** Leave is available at the time of the birth or adoption, not substantially earlier or later. *See* Guidelines On the Massachusetts Maternity Leave Act (available on the MCAD website).

156. *See* 29 CFR §825.115.

157. *See* 29 CFR §825.302(e).

158. *See* Guidelines on the Massachusetts Maternity Leave Act, Question 6 (available on the MCAD website).

159. 19 U.S.C. §651 et seq.

160. 29 CFR §§1910-1990 (available on the OSHA website).

161. 29 CFR §1910.1200.

162. 29 CFR §1977.12.

163. Whirlpool Corp. v. Marshall, 445 U.S. 1 (1980).

164. 49 U.S.C. §31105(a)(1)(B).

165. *See* 49 CFR §392.3; Yellow Freight Systems, Inc. v. Reich, 8 F.3d 980, 984-986 (4th Cir. 1993).

166. **NOTE:** A 2007 amendment added punitive damages to STAA remedies.

167. 29 CFR §1910.95(b)(1).

168. 29 CFR §1910.132(h).

169. *See* 29 CFR §1910.134(a)(1).

170. 29 U.S.C. §151 (paragraph 5).

171. M.G.L. ch.150E, §4 (paragraph 6).

172. 29 U.S.C. §401 et seq.

173. NLRB v. J. Weingarten, Inc., 420 U.S. 251 (1975). **NOTE:** Weingarten rights apply in the public sector. *See* Town of Hudson v. Labor Relations Comm., 69 Mass.App.Ct. 549 (2007). **FURTHER NOTE:** The National Labor Relations Board has gone back and forth on whether Weingarten applies to nonunion employees. Its most recent decision denies representation. IBM Corp., 341 NLRB 1288 (2004).

174. M.G.L. ch.151B, §1 et seq.

175. 42 U.S.C. §2000e.

176. *See* 804 CMR §1.10(2).

177. 42 U.S.C. §2000e-1(a); M.G.L. ch.151B, §1(5).

178. **NOTE:** In this respect, Title VII is stricter than FEPA, which allows race to qualify as a bona fide occupational qualification. *See* M.G.L. ch.151B, §4(1).

179. Griggs v. Duke Power Co., 401 U.S. 424 (1971).

180. 42 U.S.C. §2000e-2(h).

181. *See* Lynn Teacher's Union, Local 1037, v. MCAD, 406 Mass. 515,

525 (1990) ("[T]he Legislature did not intend to screen bona fide seniority systems from the scrutiny of all of the Commonwealth's antidiscrimination laws.").

182. 8 U.S.C. §§1324a and b. **NOTE:** IRCA allows employers to favor U.S. citizens and nationals over equally qualified aliens when filling positions. 8 U.S.C. §1324b(a)(4).

183. **NOTE:** SSA is currently reevaluating its no-match program. Letters were not sent out in 2007.

184. *See* 29 CFR §1606.7.

185. *See* Danco, Inc. v. Wal-Mart Stores, Inc., 178 F.3d 8, 13-14 (1st Cir. 1999).

186. 8 U.S.C. §1324b(a)(6).

187. United Auto Workers v. Johnson Controls, Inc., 499 U.S. 187, 206 (1991).

188. *See* 804 CMR §3.02.

189. LeBoeuf v. Ramsey, 503 F.Supp. 747 (D.Mass. 1980).

190. Davis v. Richmond, Fredericksburg and Potomac R. Co., 803 F.2d 1322, 1327-28 (4th Cir. 1986). *See also* Kilgo v. Bowman Transp.Co., 789 F.2d 859 (11th Cir. 1986) (one year over-the-road experience for truck driver).

191. 29 U.S.C. §206(d).

192. M.G.L. ch.149, §105A. **NOTE:** The law is applicable to employers without regard to size.

193. *See* Jancey v. School Committee of Everett, 421 Mass. 482, 486-91 (1995) (cafeteria workers and custodians did not perform work of comparable character because substantive content of the jobs being compared did not share common characteristics); Silvestris v. Tantasqua Regional School

District, 446 Mass. 756, 771-757 (2006) (seniority includes experience in prior employment).

194. *See* Pennsylvania State Police v. Suders, 542 U.S. 129 (2004); Goss v. Exxon Office Systems Co., 747 F.2nd 585 (3rd Cir. 1984). **NOTE:** Adverse working conditions must be unusually aggravated or amount to a continuous pattern of hostile conduct.

195. *See* Miller v. Dept. of Corrections, 115 P.3d 77, 88-90 (Cal. Sup. Ct. 2005). *See also* Office of Legal Counsel, Policy Guidance on Employer Liability Under Title VII for Sexual Favoritism, EEOC Policy Statement No. N-915-048, Section C (January 12, 1990).

196. M.G.L. ch.151B, §3A.

197. *See* College-Town, Div. of Interco, Inc. v. MCAD, 400 Mass. 156, 165 (1987).

198. M.G.L. ch.214, §1C (300-day statute of limitations).

199. *See* Haskins v. Secretary of Health and Human Services, 35 FEP 256 (W.D.Mo. 1984).

200. *See* Tavora v. New York Mercantile Exch., 101 F.3d 907, 908 (2nd Cir. 1996); Fountain v. Safeway Stores, 555 F.2d 753, 754 (9th Cir. 1977).

201. Millett v. Lutco, Inc., 2001 WL 1602800 (MCAD 2001). *See also* Price Waterhouse v. Hopkins, 490 U.S. 228, 250 (1989) (illegal to treat female employee adversely for failing to conform to stereotypical gender norms).

202. 29 U.S.C. §621 et seq. (applicable to employers with twenty or more workers)

203. **NOTE:** A state criminal statute, applicable to employers of all sizes, forbids employers from dis-

missing or refusing to hire employees because they are over age 40. M.G.L. ch.149, §24A. Punishment is a $500 fine.

204. 804 CMR §3.02. **NOTE:** After hiring, employers may ascertain the age of employees to comply with state and federal record-keeping requirements.

205. **NOTE:** See page 54 for requirement of a conditional job offer prior to a medical examination.

206. **NOTE:** M.G.L. ch 32, §1 in its definition of "maximum age" establishes a mandatory retirement age of 65 for police officers, firefighters, correctional officers, and certain other public safety personnel.

207. **NOTE:** Federal rules mandate retirement for commercial airline pilots at age 65 and air traffic controllers at age 56.

208. Smith v. City of Jackson, Mississippi, 544 U.S. 228, 240-243 (2005). **NOTE:** The Court was influenced by language in the ADEA which is not present in the Massachusetts Fair Employment Practices Act (FEPA). Massachusetts courts have not indicated whether they will follow *Smith*.

209. 29 CFR §1625.32 (applicable to comparable state-sponsored health benefit plans).

210. 42 U.S.C. §12101 et seq.

211. *See* Dahill v. Police Dept. of Boston, 434 Mass. 233, 240, n.20 (2001).

212. *See* MCAD v. Town of Winthrop Cemetery Dept., 2003 WL 22056884 *6, (MCAD 2003) ("Complainant's back injury would not ordinarily be a qualifying handicap within the mean-

ing of M.G.L. ch.151B, because of its temporary nature.... However, because the injury was ultimately determined to be compensable under workers' compensation, complainant is deemed a qualified handicapped person within the meaning of c.151B provided he is able to perform the essential functions of the job with or without a reasonable accommodation.").

213. **NOTE:** Individuals do not have to mention the ADA or use the term "reasonable accommodation." All that is necessary is a request for a work adjustment for a reason related to a medical condition.

214. **NOTE:** The "essential functions" of a job are those functions that must necessarily be performed by the employee in order to accomplish a position's primary objectives. See MCAD Disability Discrimination Guidelines, §II(B).

215. **NOTE:** An employer must first consider whether there is a reasonable accommodation that will allow an employee to remain in his or her current position; only if the answer is no may it insist on reassignment. *See* 29 CFR §1630 app. 1630.2(0).

216. 42 U.S.C. §12111(9)(B). **NOTE:** FEPA does not require reassignments. Russell v. Cooley Dickinson Hospital, Inc., 437 Mass. 443, 454 (2002). This disadvantages employees whose employers are too small (fewer than fifteen employees) to come under ADA jurisdiction. **FURTHER NOTE:** The federal courts disagree over whether an employer must reassign a qualified disabled employee to a vacant position where this would violate a company policy of hiring the

most qualified candidate. *Compare* Smith v. Midland Brake, Inc., 180 F.3d 1154, 1164–65 (10th Cir. 1999) (reassignment required) *with* EEOC v. Humiston-Keeling, Inc., 227 F.3d 1024, 1027–28 (7th Cir. 2000) (reassignment not required).

217. *See* U.S. Airways, Inc. v. Barnett, 535 U.S. 391, 402-406 (2002).

218. Turco v. Hoechst Celanese Corp., 101 F.3d 1090, 1094 (5th Cir. 1996).

219. *See* MCAD v. Massachusetts Bay Transportation Authority, 2003 WL 23018197 *2-3 (MCAD); Johansson v. Massachusetts Com'n Against Discrimination, 69 Mass.App.Ct. 1113 (2007).

220. MCAD Guidelines: Employment Discrimination on the Basis of Handicap, Section IIA.5. *See* School Committee of Norton v. Massachusetts Com'n Against Discrimination, 63 Mass.App.Ct. 839, 845 (2005) (duty to accommodate cafeteria worker with 25-pound lifting restriction).

221. *See* Cleveland v. Policy Management Sys. Corp., 526 U.S. 795, 803-805 (1999) (SSDI); Russell v. Cooley Dickinson Hospital, Inc., 437 Mass. 443, 451-453 (2002) (workers' compensation).

222. *See* Garcia-Ayala v. Lederle Paraenteral, Inc., 212 F.3d 638, 645-650 (1st Cir. 2000).

223. Mitchell v. Mal's Service Center, 2006 WL 3612861 *4 (MCAD).

224. 42 U.S.C. §12114(c)(4).

225. **NOTE:** The maximum benefit rate is 57.5 percent of the statewide average weekly wage as of October 1 each year.

226. **NOTE:** The claimant must contribute over half of the support of the child. If both parents are unemployed, only one can collect the allowance. Children age 18 and older can qualify as dependents if they are disabled, or, if under 25, in school fulltime. The allowance can total no more than half of the weekly benefit rate.

227. **NOTE:** Instead of paying contributions, governmental and non-profit employers can reimburse DUA dollar-for-dollar for unemployment benefits paid to their workers.

228. M.G.L. ch.151A, §58A (paragraph 3).

229. **NOTE:** A plant closing is defined as a permanent cessation or reduction of business at a facility of at least fifty employees which results or will result in the permanent separation of at least 50 percent of the employees of a facility or facilities. M.G.L. ch.151A, §1(r)(3) (paragraph 2).

230. **NOTE:** After fifteen weeks, the DUA expects claimants to accept lower-paying jobs.

231. M.G.L. ch.151A, §25(b).

232. *See* Reed National Corp. v. Director of DES, 393 Mass. 721 (1985). **NOTE:** A walkout by a department or job classification may be ruled a stoppage even if operations are maintained by farming out struck work. *See* General Electric Co. v. Dir. of DES, 349 Mass. 358, 364-365 (1965).

233. **NOTE:** Strike benefits are not considered remuneration under the UI law. Worcester Telegram Pub. Co. v. Director of DES, 347 Mass. 505, 514 (1964).

234. M.G.L ch.151A, §25(b) (second to last paragraph).

235. **NOTE:** Employers often present hearsay evidence at DUA hearings. For example, a personnel manager may recount an incident of insubordination reported to her by a supervisor. Claimants have had success arguing that, unless corroborated by an eyewitness, hearsay evidence is insufficient to support a disqualification. *See* Sinclair v. Director of DES, 331 Mass. 101, 103–104 (1954); City of Woburn v. Commissioner of Dept. of Employment & Training, 65 Mass.App.Ct. 1106 (2005).

236. M.G.L. ch.151A, §25(e) (paragraph 8).

237. **NOTE:** Pay continuation provided by state law.

238. **NOTE:** Covered by a federal workers' compensation program.

239. **NOTE:** Civil suits allowed.

240. MG.L. ch.152, §1(7A).

241. M.G.L. ch.152, §1(1) (paragraph 2).

242. **NOTE:** An employee can collect partial incapacity benefits for ten years if he or she develops a life-threatening physical condition, contracts a permanently disabling occupational disease, or loses 75 percent or more of the use of an eye, arm, leg, or foot. The period is reduced to seven years if the employee receives three years of TTI benefits.

243. M.G.L. ch.152, §41. **NOTE:** Although Section 42 of the compensation act requires a written communication, Section 44 makes knowledge of the injury by the insured or the insurer a substitute for written notice. Knowledge includes oral notice as well as observation of an injury or its symptoms. *See* Davidson's Case, 338 Mass. 228, 231 (1958) (soon after truck accident, employer agent observed claimant limping). Want of notice may also be excused if the insurer is not prejudiced.

244. M.G.L. ch.152, §75A.

245. M.G.L. ch.152, §75B.

246. Medellin's Case (2003) (available on DIA website).

Index